Mary Hartwell Catherwood

The Chase of Saint-Castin

And other Stories of the French in the New World

Mary Hartwell Catherwood

The Chase of Saint-Castin
And other Stories of the French in the New World

ISBN/EAN: 9783743336841

Manufactured in Europe, USA, Canada, Australia, Japa

Cover: Foto ©ninafisch / pixelio.de

Manufactured and distributed by brebook publishing software (www.brebook.com)

Mary Hartwell Catherwood

The Chase of Saint-Castin

CONTENTS.

	PAGE
The Chase of Saint-Castin	1
The Beauport Loup-Garou	50
The Mill at Petit Cap	84
Wolfe's Cove	105
The Windigo	147
The Kidnaped Bride	190
Pontiac's Lookout	225

THE CHASE OF SAINT-CASTIN.

The waiting April woods, sensitive in every leafless twig to spring, stood in silence and dim nightfall around a lodge. Wherever a human dwelling is set in the wilderness, it becomes, by the very humility of its proportions, a prominent and aggressive point. But this lodge of bark and poles was the color of the woods, and nearly escaped intruding as man's work. A glow lighted the top, revealing the faint azure of smoke which rose straight upward in the cool, clear air.

Such a habitation usually resounded at nightfall with Indian noises, especially if the day's hunting had been good. The mossy rocks lying around were not more silent than the inmates of this lodge. You could hear the Penobscot River foaming along its uneasy bed half a mile eastward. The poles showed freshly cut disks of yellow at the top; and though the bark coverings were such movables as any Indian household carried, they were newly fastened to their present support. This was plainly the night encampment of a traveling party, and two French hunters and their attendant Abenaquis recognized that, as it barred their trail to the river. An odor of roasted meat was wafted out like an invitation to them.

"Excellent, Saint-Castin," pronounced the older Frenchman. "Here is another of your wilderness surprises. No wonder you prefer an enchanted land to the rough mountains around Béarn. I shall never go back to France myself."

"Stop, La Hontan!" The young man restrained his guest from plunging into the wigwam with a headlong gesture recently learned and practiced with delight. "I never saw this lodge before."

"Did you not have it set up here for the night?"

"No; it is not mine. Our Abenaquis are going to build one for us nearer the river."

"I stay here," observed La Hontan. "Supper is ready, and adventures are in the air."

"But this is not a hunter's lodge. You see that our very dogs understand they have no business here. Come on."

"Come on, without seeing who is hid herein? No. I begin to think it is something thou wouldst conceal from me. I go in; and if it be a bear trap, I cheerfully perish."

The young Frenchman stood resting the end of his gun on sodden leaves. He felt vexed at La Hontan. But that inquisitive nobleman stooped to lift the tent flap, and the young man turned toward his waiting Indians and talked a moment in Abenaqui, when they went on in the direction of the river, carrying game and camp luggage. They thought, as he did, that this might be a lodge with which no man ought to meddle. The daughter of Madockawando, the chief, was known to be coming from her winter retreat. Every Abenaqui in the tribe stood in awe of the maid. She did not rule them as a wise woman, but lived apart from them as a superior spirit.

Baron La Hontan, on all fours, intruded his gay face on the inmates of the lodge. There were three of them. His palms encountered a carpet of hemlock twigs, which spread around a central fire to the circular wall, and was made sweetly odorous by the heat. A thick couch of the twigs was piled up beyond the fire, and there sat an Abenaqui girl in her winter dress of furs. She was so white-skinned that she startled La Hontan as an apparition of Europe. He got but one black-eyed glance. She drew her blanket over her head. The group had doubtless heard the conference outside, but ignored it with reticent gravity. The hunter of the lodge was on his heels by the embers, toasting collops of meat for the blanketed princess; and an Etchemin woman, the other inmate, took one from his hand,

and paused, while dressing it with salt, to gaze at the Frenchman.

La Hontan had not found himself distasteful to northwestern Indian girls. It was the first time an aboriginal face had ever covered itself from exposure to his eyes. He felt the sudden respect which nuns command, even in those who scoff at their visible consecration. The usual announcement made on entering a cabin — "I come to see this man," or "I come to see that woman," — he saw was to be omitted in addressing this strangely civilized Indian girl.

"Mademoiselle," said Baron La Hontan in very French Abenaqui, rising to one knee, and sweeping the twigs with the brim of his hat as he pulled it off, "the Baron de Saint-Castin of Pentegoet, the friend of your chief Madockawando, is at your lodge door, tired and chilled from a long hunt. Can you not permit him to warm at your fire?"

The Abenaqui girl bowed her covered head. Her woman companion passed the permission on, and the hunter made it audible by a grunt of assent. La Hontan backed nimbly out, and seized the waiting man by the leg. The main portion of the baron was in the darkening April woods, but his perpendicular soles stood behind the flap within the lodge.

"Enter, my child," he whispered in excitement. "A warm fire, hot collops, a black eye to be coaxed out of a blanket, and full permission given to enjoy all. What, man! Out of countenance at thought of facing a pretty squaw, when you have three keeping house with you at the fort?"

"Come out, La Hontan," whispered back Saint-Castin, on his part grasping the elder's arm. "It is Madockawando's daughter."

"The red nun thou hast told me about? The saints be praised! But art thou sure?"

"How can I be sure? I have never seen her myself. But I judge from her avoiding your impudent eye. She does not like to be looked at."

"It was my mentioning the name of Saint-Castin of Pentegoet that made her whip her head under the blanket. I see, if I am to keep my reputation in the woods, I shall have to withdraw from your company."

"Withdraw your heels from this lodge," replied Saint-Castin impatiently. "You will embroil me with the tribe."

"Why should it embroil you with the tribe," argued the merry sitter, "if we warm our heels decently at this ready fire until the Indians light our own? Any Christian, white or red, would grant us that privilege."

"If I enter with you, will you come out with me as soon as I make you a sign?"

"Doubt it not," said La Hontan, and he eclipsed himself directly.

Though Saint-Castin had been more than a year in Acadia, this was the first time he had ever seen Madockawando's daughter. He knew it was that elusive being, on her way from her winter retreat to the tribe's summer fishing station near the coast.

Father Petit, the priest of this woodland parish, spoke of her as one who might in time found a house of holy women amidst the license of the wilderness.

Saint-Castin wanted to ask her pardon for entering; but he sat without a sound. Some power went out from that silent shape far stronger than the hinted beauty of girlish ankle and arm. The glow of brands lighted the lodge, showing the bark seams on its poles. Pale smoke and the pulse of heat quivered betwixt him and a presence which, by some swift contrast, made his face burn at the recollection of his household at Pentegoet. He had seen many good women in his life, with the patronizing tolerance which men bestow on unpiquant things that are harmless; and he did not understand why her hiding should stab him like a reproach. She hid from all common eyes. But his were not common eyes. Saint-Castin felt impatient at getting no recognition from a girl, saint though she might be, whose tribe he had actually adopted.

The blunt-faced Etchemin woman, once a prisoner brought from northern Acadia, now the companion of Madockawando's daughter, knew her duty to the strangers, and gave them food as rapidly as the hunter could broil it. The hunter was a big-legged, small-headed Abenaqui, with knees overtopping his tuft of hair when he squatted on his heels. He looked like a man whose emaciated trunk and arms had been taken possession of by colossal legs and feet. This singular deformity made him the best hunter in his tribe. He tracked game with a sweep of great beams as tireless as the tread of a modern steamer. The little sense in his head was woodcraft. He thought of nothing but taking and dressing game.

Saint-Castin barely tasted the offered meat; but La Hontan enjoyed it unabashed, warming himself while he ate, and avoiding any chance of a hint from his friend that the meal should be cut short.

"My child," he said in lame Abenaqui to the Etchemin woman, while his sly regard dwelt on the blanket-robed statue opposite, "I wish you the best of gifts, a good husband."

The Etchemin woman heard him in such silence as one perhaps brings from making a long religious retreat, and forbore to explain that she already had the best of gifts, and was the wife of the big-legged hunter.

"I myself had an aunt who never married," warned La Hontan. "She was an excellent woman, but she turned like fruit withered in the ripening. The fantastic airs of her girlhood clung to her. She was at a disadvantage among the married, and young people passed her by as an experiment that had failed. So she was driven to be very religious; but prayers are cold comfort for the want of a bouncing family."

If the Etchemin woman had absorbed from her mistress a habit of meditation which shut out the world, Saint-Castin had not. He gave La Hontan the sign to move before him out of the lodge, and no choice but to obey it, crowding the reluctant and comfortable man into undignified attitudes. La Hontan saw that he had taken offense. There was no accounting for the humors of those disbanded soldiers of the Carignan-Salières, though Saint-Castin was usually a gentle fellow. They spread out their sensitive military honor over every inch of their new seigniories; and if you chucked the wrong little Indian or habitant's naked baby under the chin, you might unconsciously stir up war in the mind of your host. La Hontan was glad he was directly leaving Acadia. He was fond of Saint-Castin. Few people could approach that young man without feeling the charm which made the Indians adore him. But any one who establishes himself in the woods loses touch with the light manners of civilization; his very vices take on an air of brutal candor.

Next evening, however, both men were merry by the hall fire at Pentegoet over their parting cup. La Hontan was returning to Quebec. A vessel waited the tide at the Penobscot's mouth, a bay which the Indians call "bad harbor."

The long, low, and irregular building which Saint-Castin had constructed as his baronial seat was as snug as the governor's castle at Quebec. It was only one story high, and the small square windows were set under the eaves, so outsiders could not look in. Saint-Castin's enemies said he built thus to hide his deeds; but Father Petit himself could see how excellent a plan it was for defense. A holding already claimed by the encroaching English needed loop-holes, not windows. The fort surrounding the house was also well adapted to its situation. Twelve cannon guarded the bastions. All the necessary buildings, besides a chapel with a bell, were within the walls, and a deep well insured a supply of water. A garden and fruit orchard were laid out opposite the fort, and encompassed by palisades.

The luxury of the house consisted in an abundant use of crude, unpolished material. Though built grotesquely of stone and wood intermingled, it had the solid dignity of that rugged coast. A chimney spacious as a crater let smoke and white ashes upward, and sections of trees smouldered on Saint-Castin's hearth. An Indian girl, ruddy from high living, and wearing the brightest stuffs imported from France, sat on the floor at the hearth corner. This was the usual night scene at Pentegoet. Candle and firelight shone on her, on oak timbers, and settles made of unpeeled balsam, on plate and glasses which always heaped a table with ready food and drink, on moose horns and gun racks, on stores of books, on festoons of wampum, and usually on a dozen figures beside Saint-Castin. The other rooms in the house were mere tributaries to this baronial presence chamber. Madockawando and the dignitaries of the Abenaqui tribe made it their council hall, the white sagamore presiding. They were superior to rude western nations. It was Saint-Castin's plan to make a strong principality here, and to unite his people in a compact state. He lavished his inherited money upon them. Whatever they wanted from Saint-Castin they got, as from a father. On their part, they poured the wealth of the woods upon him. Not a beaver skin went out of Acadia except through his hands. The traders of New France grumbled at his profits and monopoly, and the English of New England claimed his seigniory. He stood on debatable ground, in dangerous times, trying to mould an independent nation. The Abenaquis did not know that a king of France had been reared on Saint-Castin's native mountains, but they believed that a human divinity had.

Their permanent settlement was about the fort, on land he had paid for, but held in common with them. They went to their winter's hunting or their summer's fishing from Pentegoet. It was the seat of power. The cannon protected fields and a town of lodges which Saint-Castin meant to convert into a town of stone and hewed wood houses as soon as the aboriginal nature conformed itself to such stability. Even now the village had left home and gone into the woods again. The Abenaqui women were busy there, inserting tubes of bark in pierced maple-trees, and troughs caught the flow of ascending sap. Kettles boiled over fires in the bald spaces, incense of the forest's very heart rising from them and sweetening the air. All day Indian children raced from one mother's fire to another, or dipped unforbidden cups of hands into the brimming troughs; and at night they lay down among the dogs, with their heels to the blaze, watching these lower constellations blink through the woods until their eyes swam into unconsciousness. It was good weather for making maple sugar. In the mornings hoar frost or light snows silvered the world, disappearing as soon as the sun touched them, when the bark of every tree leaked moisture. This was festive labor compared with planting the fields, and drew the men, also.

The morning after La Hontan sailed, Saint-Castin went out and skirted this widespread sugar industry like a spy. The year before, he had moved heartily from fire to fire, hailed and entertained by every red manufacturer. The unrest of spring was upon him. He had brought many conveniences among the Abenaquis, and taught them some civilized arts. They were his adopted people. But he felt a sudden separateness from them, like the loneliness of his early boyhood.

Saint-Castin was a good hunter. He had more than once watched a slim young doe stand gazing curiously at him, and had not startled it by a breath. Therefore he was able to become a stump behind the tree which Madockawando's daughter sought with her sap pail. Usually he wore buckskins, in the free and easy life of Pentegoet. But he had put on his Carignan-Salières uniform, filling its boyish outlines with his full man's figure. He would not on any account have had La Hontan see him thus gathering the light of the open woods on military finery. He felt ashamed of returning to it, and could not account for his own impulses; and when he saw Madockawando's daughter walking unconsciously toward him as toward a trap, he drew his bright surfaces entirely behind the column of the tree.

She had taken no part in this festival of labor for several years. She moved among the women still in solitude, not one of them feeling at liberty to draw near her except as she encouraged them. The Abenaquis were not a polygamous tribe, but they enjoyed the freedom of the woods. Squaws who had made several experimental marriages since this young celibate began her course naturally felt rebuked by her standards, and preferred stirring kettles to meeting her. It was not so long since the princess had been a hoiden among them, abounding in the life which rushes to extravagant action. Her juvenile whoops scared the birds. She rode astride of saplings, and played pranks on solemn old warriors and the medicine-man. Her body grew into suppleness and beauty. As for her spirit, the women of the tribe knew very little about it. They saw none of her struggles. In childhood she was ashamed of the finer nature whose wants found no answer in her world. It was anguish to look into the faces of her kindred and friends as into the faces of hounds who live, it is true, but a lower life, made up of chasing and eating. She wondered why she was created different from them. A loyalty of race constrained her sometimes to imitate them; but it was imitation; she could not be a savage. Then Father Petit came, preceding Saint-Castin, and set up his altar and built his chapel. The Abenaqui girl was converted as soon as she looked in at the door and saw the gracious image of Mary lifted up to be her pattern of womanhood. Those silent and terrible days, when she lost interest in the bustle of living, and felt an awful homesickness for some unknown good, passed entirely away. Religion opened an invisible world. She sprang toward it, lying on the wings of her spirit and gazing forever above. The minutest observances of the Church were learned with an exactness which delighted a priest who had not too many encouragements. Finally, she begged her father to let her make a winter retreat to some place near the headwaters of the Penobscot. When the hunters were abroad, it did them no harm to remember there was a maid in a wilderness cloister praying for the good of her people; and when they were fortunate, they believed in the material advantage of her prayers. Nobody thought of searching out her hidden cell, or of asking the big-legged hunter and his wife to tell its mysteries. The dealer with invisible spirits commanded respect in Indian minds before the priest came.

Madockawando's daughter was of a lighter color than most of her tribe, and finer in her proportions, though they were a well-made people. She was the highest expression of unadulterated Abenaqui blood. She set her sap pail down by the trough, and Saint-Castin shifted silently to watch her while she dipped the juice. Her eyelids were lowered. She had well-marked brows, and the high cheek-bones were lost in a general acquiline rosiness. It was a girl's face, modest and sweet, that he saw; reflecting the society of holier beings than the one behind the tree. She had no blemish of sunken temples or shrunk features, or the glaring aspect of a devotee. Saint-Castin was a good Catholic, but he did not like fanatics. It was as if the choicest tree in the forest had been flung open, and a perfect woman had stepped out, whom no other man's eye had seen. Her throat was round, and at the base of it, in the little hollow where women love to nestle ornaments, hung the cross of her rosary, which she wore twisted about her neck. The beads were large and white, and the cross was ivory. Father Petit had furnished them, blessed for their purpose, to his incipient abbess, but Saint-Castin noticed how they set off the dark rosiness of her skin. The collar of her fur dress was pushed back, for the day was warm, like an autumn day when there is no wind. A luminous smoke which magnified the light hung between treetops and zenith. The nakedness of the swelling forest let heaven come strangely close to the ground. It was like standing on a mountain plateau in a gray dazzle of clouds.

Madockawando's daughter dipped her pail full of the clear water. The appreciative motion of her eyelashes and the placid lines of her face told how she enjoyed the limpid plaything. But Saint-Castin understood well that she had not come out to boil sap entirely for the love of it. Father Petit believed the time was ripe for her ministry to the Abenaqui women. He had intimated to the seignior what land might be convenient for the location of a convent. The community was now to be drawn around her. Other girls must take vows when she did. Some half-covered children, who stalked her wherever she went, stood like terra-cotta images at a distance and waited for her next movement.

The girl had just finished her dipping when she looked up and met the steady gaze of Saint-Castin. He was in an anguish of dread that she would run. But her startled eyes held his image while three changes passed over her, — terror and recognition and disapproval. He stepped more into view, a white-and-gold apparition, which scattered the Abenaqui children to their mothers' camp-fires.

"I am Saint-Castin," he said.

"Yes, I have many times seen you, sagamore."

Her voice, shaken a little by her heart, was modulated to such softness that the liquid gutturals gave him a distinct new pleasure.

"I want to ask your pardon for my friend's rudeness, when you warmed and fed us in your lodge."

"I did not listen to him." Her fingers sought the cross on her neck. She seemed to threaten a prayer which might stop her ears to Saint-Castin.

"He meant no discourtesy. If you knew his good heart, you would like him."

"I do not like men." She made a calm statement of her peculiar tastes.

"Why?" inquired Saint-Castin.

Madockawando's daughter summoned her reasons from distant vistas of the woods, with meditative dark eyes. Evidently her dislike of men had no element of fear or of sentimental avoidance.

"I cannot like them," she apologized, declining to set forth her reasons. "I wish they would always stay away from me."

"Your father and the priest are men."

"I know it," admitted the girl, with a deep breath like commiseration. "They cannot help it; and our Etchemin's husband, who keeps the lodge supplied with meat, he cannot help it, either, any more than he can his deformity. But there is grace for men," she added. "They may, by repenting of their sins and living holy lives, finally save their souls."

Saint-Castin repented of his sins that moment, and tried to look contrite.

"In some of my books," he said, "I read of an old belief held by people on the other side of the earth. They thought our souls were born into the world a great many times, now in this body, and now in that. I feel as if you and I had been friends in some other state."

The girl's face seemed to flare toward him as flame is blown, acknowledging the claim he made upon her; but the look passed like an illusion, and she said seriously, "The sagamore should speak to Father Petit. This is heresy."

Madockawando's daughter stood up, and took her pail by the handle.

"Let me carry it," said Saint-Castin.

Her lifted palm barred his approach.

"I do not like men, sagamore. I wish them to keep away from me."

"But that is not Christian," he argued.

"It cannot be unchristian: the priest would lay me under penance for it."

"Father Petit is a lenient soul."

With the simplicity of an angel who would not be longer hindered by mundane society, she took up her pail, saying, "Good-day, sagamore," and swept on across the dead leaves.

Saint-Castin walked after her.

"Go back," commanded Madockawando's daughter, turning.

The officer of the Carignan-Salières regiment halted, but did not retreat.

"You must not follow me, sagamore," she remonstrated, as with a child. "I cannot talk to you."

"You must let me talk to you," said Saint-Castin. "I want you for my wife."

She looked at him in a way that made his face scorch. He remembered the year wife, the half-year wife, and the two-months wife at Pentegoet. These three squaws whom he had allowed to form his household, and had taught to boil the pot au feu, came to him from many previous experimental marriages. They were externals of his life, much as hounds, boats, or guns. He could give them all rich dowers, and divorce them easily any day to a succeeding line of legal Abenaqui husbands. The lax code of the wilderness was irresistible to a Frenchman; but he was near enough in age and in texture of soul to this noble pagan to see at once, with her eyesight, how he had degraded the very vices of her people.

"Before the sun goes down," vowed Saint-Castin, "there shall be nobody in my house but the two Etchemin slave men that your father gave me."

The girl heard of his promised reformation without any kindling of the spirit.

"I am not for a wife," she answered him, and walked on with the pail.

Again Saint-Castin followed her, and took the sap pail from her hand. He set it aside on the leaves, and folded his arms. The blood came and went in his face. He was not used to pleading with women. They belonged to him easily, like his natural advantages over barbarians in a new world. The slopes of the Pyrenees bred strong-limbed men, cautious in policy, striking and bold in figure and countenance. The English themselves have borne witness to his fascinations. Manhood had darkened only the surface of his skin, a milk-white cleanness breaking through it like the outflushing of some inner purity. His eyes and hair had a golden beauty. It would have been strange if he had not roused at least a degree of comradeship in the aboriginal woman living up to her highest aspirations.

"I love you. I have thought of you, of nobody but you, even when I behaved the worst. You have kept yourself hid from me, while I have been thinking about you ever since I came to Acadia. You are the woman I want to marry."

Madockawando's daughter shook her head. She had patience with his fantastic persistence, but it annoyed her.

"I am not for a wife," she repeated. "I do not like men."

"Is it that you do not like me?"

"No," she answered sincerely, probing her mind for the truth. "You yourself are different from our Abenaqui men."

"Then why do you make me unhappy?"

"I do not make you unhappy. I do not even think of you."

Again she took to her hurried course, forgetting the pail of sap. Saint-Castin seized it, and once more followed her.

"I beg that you will kiss me," he pleaded, trembling.

The Abenaqui girl laughed aloud.

"Does the sagamore think he is an object of veneration, that I should kiss him?"

"But will you not at least touch your lips to my forehead?"

"No. I touch my lips to holy things."

"You do not understand the feeling I have."

"No, I do not understand it. If you talked every day, it would do no good. My thoughts are different."

Saint-Castin gave her the pail, and looked her in the eyes.

"Perhaps you will some time understand," he said. "I lived many wild years before I did."

She was so glad to leave him behind that her escape was like a backward blow, and he did not make enough allowance for the natural antagonism of a young girl. Her beautiful free motion was something to watch. She was a convert whose penances were usually worked out afoot, for Father Petit knew better than to shut her up.

Saint-Castin had never dreamed there were such women. She was like a nymph out of a tree, without human responsiveness, yet with round arms and waist and rosy column of neck, made to be helplessly adored. He remembered the lonesome moods of his early youth. They must have been a premonition of his fate in falling completely under the spell of an unloving woman.

Saint-Castin took a roundabout course, and went to Madockawando's lodge, near the fort. All the members of the family, except the old chief, were away at the sugar-making. The great Abenaqui's dignity would not allow him to drag in fuel to the fire, so he squatted nursing the ashes, and raked out a coal to light tobacco for himself and Saint-Castin. The white sagamore had never before come in full uniform to a private talk, and it was necessary to smoke half an hour before a word could be said.

There was a difference between the chatter of civilized men and the deliberations of barbarians. With La Hontan, the Baron de Saint-Castin would have led up to his business by a long prelude on other subjects. With Madockawando, he waited until the tobacco had mellowed both their spirits, and then said, —

"Father, I want to marry your daughter in the French way, with priest and contract, and make her the Baroness de Saint-Castin."

Madockawando, on his part, smoked the matter fairly out. He put an arm on the sagamore's shoulder, and lamented the extreme devotion of his daughter. It was a good religion which the black-robed father had brought among the Abenaquis, but who had ever heard of a woman's refusing to look at men before that religion came? His own child, when she was at home with the tribe, lived as separate from the family and as independently as a war-chief. In his time, the women dressed game and carried the children and drew sledges. What would happen if his daughter began to teach them, in a house by themselves, to do nothing but pray? Madockawando repeated that his son, the sagamore, and his father, the priest, had a good religion, but they might see for themselves what the Abenaqui tribe would come to when the women all set up for medicine squaws. Then there was his daughter's hiding in winter to make what she called her retreats, and her proposing to take a new name from some of the priest's okies or saint-spirits, and to be called "Sister."

"I will never call my own child 'Sister,'" vowed Madockawando. "I could be a better Christian myself, if Father Petit had not put spells on her."

The two conspirators against Father Petit's proposed nunnery felt grave and wicked, but they encouraged one another in iniquity. Madockawando smiled in bronze wrinkles when Saint-Castin told him about the proposal in the woods. The proper time for courtship was evening, as any Frenchman who had lived a year with the tribe ought to know; but when one considered the task he had undertaken, any time was suitable; and the chief encouraged him with full consent. A French marriage contract was no better than an Abenaqui marriage contract in Madockawando's eyes; but if Saint-Castin could bind up his daughter for good, he would be glad of it.

The chapel of saplings and bark which first sheltered Father Petit's altar had been abandoned when Saint-Castin built a substantial one of stone and timber within the fortress walls, and hung in its little tower a bell, which the most reluctant Abenaqui must hear at mass time. But as it is well to cherish the sacred regard which man has for any spot where he has worshiped, the priest left a picture hanging on the wall above the bare chancel, and he kept the door repaired on its wooden hinges. The chapel stood beyond the forest, east of Pentegoet, and close to those battlements which form the coast line here. The tide made thunder as it rose among caverns and frothed almost at the verge of the heights. From this headland Mount Desert could be seen, leading the host of islands which go out into the Atlantic, ethereal in fog or lurid in the glare of sunset.

Madockawando's daughter tended the old chapel in summer, for she had first seen religion through its door. She wound the homely chancel rail with evergreens, and put leaves and red berries on the walls, and flowers under the sacred picture; her Etchemin woman always keeping her company. Father Petit hoped to see this rough shrine become a religious seminary, and strings of women led there every day to take, like contagion, from an abbess the instruction they took so slowly from a priest.

She and the Etchemin found it a dismal place, on their first visit after the winter retreat. She reproached herself for coming so late; but day and night an influence now encompassed Madockawando's daughter which she felt as a restraint on her freedom. A voice singing softly the love-songs of southern France often waked her from her sleep. The words she could not interpret, but the tone the whole village could, and she blushed, crowding paters on aves, until her voice sometimes became as distinct as Saint-Castin's in resolute opposition. It was so grotesque that it made her laugh. Yet to a woman the most formidable quality in a suitor is determination.

When the three girls who had constituted Saint-Castin's household at the fort passed complacently back to their own homes laden with riches, Madockawando's daughter was unreasonably angry, and felt their loss as they were incapable of feeling it for themselves. She was alien to the customs of her people. The fact pressed upon her that her people were completely bound to the white sagamore and all his deeds. Saint-Castin's sins had been open to the tribe, and his repentance was just as open. Father Petit praised him.

"My son Jean Vincent de l'Abadie, Baron de Saint-Castin, has need of spiritual aid to sustain him in the paths of virtue," said the priest impressively, " and he is seeking it."

At every church service the lax sinner was now on his knees in plain sight of the devotee; but she never looked at him. All the tribe soon knew what he had at heart, and it was told from camp-fire to camp-fire how he sat silent every night in the hall at Pentegoet, with his hair ruffled on his forehead, growing more haggard from day to day.

The Abenaqui girl did not talk with other women about what happened in the community. Dead saints crowded her mind to the exclusion of living sinners. All that she heard came by way of her companion, the stolid Etchemin, and when it was unprofitable talk it was silenced. They labored together all the chill April afternoon, bringing the chapel out of its winter desolation. The Etchemin made brooms of hemlock, and brushed down cobwebs and dust, and laboriously swept the rocky earthen floor, while the princess, standing upon a scaffold of split log benches, wiped the sacred picture and set a border of tender moss around it. It was a gaudy red print representing a pierced heart. The Indian girl kissed every sanguinary drop which dribbled down the coarse paper. Fog and salt air had given it a musty odor, and stained the edges with mildew. She found it no small labor to cover these stains, and pin the moss securely in place with thorns.

There were no windows in this chapel. A platform of hewed slabs had supported the altar; and when the princess came down, and the benches were replaced, she lifted one of these slabs, as she had often done before, to look into the earthen-floored box which they made. Little animals did not take refuge in the wind-beaten building. She often wondered that it stood; though the light materials used by aboriginal tribes, when anchored to the earth as this house was, toughly resisted wind and weather.

The Etchemin sat down on the ground, and her mistress on the platform behind the chancel rail, when everything else was done, to make a fresh rope of evergreen. The climbing and reaching and lifting had heated their faces, and the cool salt air flowed in, refreshing them. Their hands were pricked by the spiny foliage, but they labored without complaint, in unbroken meditation. A monotonous low singing of the Etchemin's kept company with the breathing of the sea. This decking of the chapel acted like music on the Abenaqui girl. She wanted to be quiet, to enjoy it.

By the time they were ready to shut the door for the night the splash of a rising tide could be heard. Fog obliterated the islands, and a bleak gray twilight, like the twilights of winter, began to dim the woods.

"The sagamore has made a new law," said the Etchemin woman, as they came in sight of the fort.

Madockawando's daughter looked at the unguarded bastions, and the chimneys of Pentegoet rising in a stack above the walls.

"What new law has the sagamore made?" she inquired.

"He says he will no more allow a man to put away his first and true wife, for he is convinced that God does not love inconstancy in men."

"The sagamore should have kept his first wife himself."

"But he says he has not yet had her," answered the Etchemin woman, glancing aside at the princess. "The sagamore will not see the end of the sugar-making to-night."

"Because he sits alone every night by his fire," said Madockawando's daughter; "there is too much talk about the sagamore. It is the end of the sugar-making that your mind is set on."

"My husband is at the camps," said the Etchemin plaintively. "Besides, I am very tired."

"Rest yourself, therefore, by tramping far to wait on your husband and keep his hands filled with warm sugar. I am tired, and I go to my lodge."

"But there is a feast in the camps, and nobody has thought of putting a kettle on in the village. I will first get your meat ready."

"No, I intend to observe a fast to-night. Go on to the camps, and serve my family there."

The Etchemin looked toward the darkening bay, and around them at those thickening hosts of invisible terrors which are yet dreaded by more enlightened minds than hers.

"No," responded the princess, "I am not afraid. Go on to the camps while you have the courage to be abroad alone."

The Etchemin woman set off at a trot, her heavy body shaking, and distance soon swallowed her. Madockawando's daughter stood still in the humid dimness before turning aside to her lodge. Perhaps the ruddy light which showed through the open fortress gate from the hall of Pentegoet gave her a feeling of security. She knew a man was there; and there was not a man anywhere else within half a league. It was the last great night of sugar-making. Not even an Abenaqui woman or child remained around the fort. Father Petit himself was at the camps to restrain riot. It would be a hard patrol for him, moving from fire to fire half the night. The master of Pentegoet rested very carelessly in his hold. It was hardly a day's sail westward to the English post of Pemaquid. Saint-Castin had really made ready for his people's spring sowing and fishing with some anxiety for their undisturbed peace. Pemaquid aggressed on him, and he seriously thought of fitting out a ship and burning Pemaquid. In that time, as in this, the strong hand upheld its own rights at any cost.

The Abenaqui girl stood under the northwest bastion, letting early night make its impressions on her. Her motionless figure, in indistinct garments, could not be seen from the river; but she discerned, rising up the path from the water, one behind the other, a row of peaked hats. Beside the hats appeared gunstocks. She had never seen any English, but neither her people nor the French showed such tops, or came stealthily up from the boat landing under cover of night. She did not stop to count them. Their business must be with Saint-Castin. She ran along the wall. The invaders would probably see her as she tried to close the gate; it had settled on its hinges, and was too heavy for her. She thought of ringing the chapel bell; but before any Abenaqui could reach the spot the single man in the fortress must be overpowered.

Saint-Castin stood on his bachelor hearth, leaning an arm on the mantel. The light shone on his buckskin fringes, his dejected shoulders, and his clean-shaven youthful face. A supper stood on the table near him, where his Etchemin servants had placed it before they trotted off to the camps. The high windows flickered, and there was not a sound in the house except the low murmur or crackle of the glowing backlog, until the door-latch clanked, and the door flew wide and was slammed shut again. Saint-Castin looked up with a frown, which changed to stupid astonishment.

Madockawando's daughter seized him by the wrist.

"Is there any way out of the fort except through the gate?"

"None," answered Saint-Castin.

"Is there no way of getting over the wall?"

"The ladder can be used."

"Run, then, to the ladder! Be quick."

"What is the matter?" demanded Saint-Castin.

The Abenaqui girl dragged on him with all her strength as he reached for the iron door-latch.

"Not that way — they will see you — they are coming from the river! Go through some other door."

"Who are coming?"

Yielding himself to her will, Saint-Castin hurried with her from room to room, and out through his kitchen, where the untidy implements of his Etchemin slaves lay scattered about. They ran past the storehouse, and he picked up a ladder and set it against the wall.

"I will run back and ring the chapel bell," panted the girl.

"Mount!" said Saint-Castin sternly; and she climbed the ladder, convinced that he would not leave her behind.

He sat on the wall and dragged the ladder up, and let it down on the outside. As they both reached the ground, he understood what enemy had nearly trapped him in his own fortress.

"The doors were all standing wide," said a cautious nasal voice, speaking English, at the other side of the wall. "Our fox hath barely sprung from cover. He must be near."

"Is not that the top of a ladder?" inquired another voice.

At this there was a rush for the gate. Madockawando's daughter ran like the wind, with Saint-Castin's hand locked in hers. She knew, by night or day, every turn of the slender trail leading to the deserted chapel. It came to her mind as the best place of refuge. They were cut off from the camps, because they must cross their pursuers on the way.

The lord of Pentegoet could hear bushes crackling behind him. The position of the ladder had pointed the direction of the chase. He laughed in his headlong flight. This was not ignominious running from foes, but a royal exhilaration. He could run all night, holding the hand that guided him. Unheeded branches struck him across the face. He shook his hair back and flew light-footed, the sweep of the magnificent body beside him keeping step. He could hear the tide boom against the headland, and the swish of its recoiling waters. The girl had her way with him. It did not occur to the officer of the Carignan regiment that he should direct the escape, or in any way oppose the will manifested for the first time in his favor. She felt for the door of the dark little chapel, and drew him in and closed it. His judgment rejected the place, but without a word he groped at her side across to the chancel rail. She lifted the loose slab of the platform, and tried to thrust him into the earthen-floored box.

"Hide yourself first," whispered Saint-Castin.

They could hear feet running on the flinty approach. The chase was so close that the English might have seen them enter the chapel.

"Get in, get in!" begged the Abenaqui girl. "They will not hurt me."

"Hide!" said Saint-Castin, thrusting her fiercely in. "Would they not carry off the core of Saint-Castin's heart if they could?"

She flattened herself on the ground under the platform, and gave him all the space at her side that the contraction of her body left clear, and he let the slab down carefully over their heads. They existed almost without breath for many minutes.

The wooden door-hinges creaked, and stumbling shins blundered against the benches.

"What is this place?" spoke an English voice. "Let some one take his tinder-box and strike a light."

"Have care," warned another. "We are only half a score in number. Our errand was to kidnap Saint-Castin from his hold, not to get ourselves ambushed by the Abenaquis."

"We are too far from the sloop now," said a third. "We shall be cut off before we get back, if we have not a care."

"But he must be in here."

"There are naught but benches and walls to hide him. This must be an idolatrous chapel where the filthy savages congregate to worship images."

"Come out of the abomination, and let us make haste back to the boat. He may be this moment marshaling all his Indians to surround us."

"Wait. Let a light first be made."

Saint-Castin and his companion heard the clicks of flint and steel; then an instant's blaze of tinder made cracks visible over their heads. It died away, the hurried, wrangling men shuffling about. One kicked the platform.

"Here is a cover," he said; but darkness again enveloped them all.

"Nothing is to be gained by searching farther," decided the majority. "Did I not tell you this Saint-Castin will never be caught? The tide will turn, and we shall get stranded among the rocks of that bay. It is better to go back without Saint-Castin than to stay and be burnt by his Abenaquis."

"But here is a loose board in some flooring," insisted the discoverer of the platform. "I will feel with the butt of my gun if there be anything thereunder."

The others had found the door, and were filing through it.

"Why not with thy knife, man?" suggested one of them.

"That is well thought of," he answered, and struck a half circle under the boards. Whether in this flourish he slashed anything he only learned by the stain on the knife, when the sloop was dropping down the bay. But the Abenaqui girl knew what he had done, before the footsteps ceased. She sat beside Saint-Castin on the platform, their feet resting on the ground within the boards. No groan betrayed him, but her arms went jealously around his body, and her searching fingers found the cut in the buckskin. She drew her blanket about him with a strength of compression that made it a ligature, and tied the corners in a knot.

"Is it deep, sagamore?"

"Not deep enough," said Saint-Castin. "It will glue me to my buckskins with a little blood, but it will not let me out of my troubles. I wonder why I ran such a race from the English? They might have had me, since they want me, and no one else does."

"I will kiss you now, sagamore," whispered the Abenaqui girl, trembling and weeping in the chaos of her broken reserve. "I cannot any longer hold out against being your wife."

She gave him her first kiss in the sacred darkness of the chapel, and under the picture of the pierced heart. And it has since been recorded of her that the Baroness de Saint-Castin was, during her entire lifetime, the best worshiped wife in Acadia.

THE BEAUPORT LOUP-GAROU.

OCTOBER dusk was bleak on the St. Lawrence, an east wind feeling along the river's surface and rocking the vessels of Sir William Phips on tawny rollers. It was the second night that his fleet sat there inactive. During that day a small ship had approached Beauport landing; but it stuck fast in the mud and became a mark for gathering Canadians until the tide rose and floated it off. At this hour all the habitants about Beauport except one, and even the Huron Indians of Lorette, were safe inside the fort walls. Cattle were driven and sheltered inland. Not a child's voice could be heard in the parish of Beauport, and not a woman's face looked through windows fronting the road leading up toward Montmorenci. Juchereau de Saint-Denis, the seignior of Beauport, had taken his tenants with him as soon as the New England invaders pushed into Quebec Basin. Only one man of the muster hid himself and stayed behind, and he was too old for military service. His seignior might lament him, but there was no woman to do so. Gaspard had not stepped off his farm for years. The priest visited him there, humoring a bent which seemed as inelastic as a vow. He had not seen the ceremonial of high mass in the cathedral of Upper Town since he was a young man.

Gaspard's farm was fifteen feet wide and a mile long. It was one of several strips lying between the St. Charles River and those heights east of Beauport which rise to Montmorenci Falls. He had his front on the greater stream, and his inland boundary among woods skirting the mountain. He raised his food and the tobacco he smoked, and braided his summer hats of straw and knitted his winter caps of wool. One suit of well-fulled woolen clothes would have lasted a habitant a lifetime.

But Gaspard had been unlucky. He lost all his family by smallpox, and the priest made him burn his clothes, and ruinously fit himself with new. There was no use in putting savings in the stocking any longer, however; the children were gone. He could only buy masses for them. He lived alone, the neighbors taking that loving interest in him which French Canadians bestow on one another.

More than once Gaspard thought he would leave his farm and go into the world. When Frontenac returned to take the paralyzed province in hand, and fight Iroquois, and repair the mistakes of the last governor, Gaspard put on his best moccasins and the red tasseled sash he wore only at Christmas. "Gaspard is going to the fort," ran along the whole row of Beauport houses. His neighbors waited for him. They all carried their guns and powder for the purpose of firing salutes to Frontenac. It was a grand day. But when Gaspard stepped out with the rest, his countenance fell. He could not tell what ailed him. His friends coaxed and pulled him; they gave him a little brandy. He sat down, and they were obliged to leave him, or miss the cannonading and fireworks themselves. From his own river front Gaspard saw the old lion's ship come to port, and, in unformed sentences, he reasoned then that a man need not leave his place to take part in the world.

Frontenac had not been back a month, and here was the New England colony of Massachusetts swarming against New France. "They may carry me away from my hearth feet first," thought Gaspard, "but I am not to be scared away from it."

Every night, before putting the bar across his door, the old habitant went out to survey the two ends of the earth typified by the road crossing his strip of farm. These were usually good moments for him. He did not groan, as at dawn, that there were no children to relieve him of labor. A noble landscape lifted on either hand from the hollow of Beauport. The ascending road went on to the little chapel of Ste. Anne de Beaupré, which for thirty years had been considered a shrine in New France. The left hand road forded the St. Charles and climbed the long slope to Quebec rock.

Gaspard loved the sounds which made home so satisfying at autumn dusk. Faint and far off he thought he could hear the lowing of his cow and calf. To remember they were exiled gave him the pang of the unusual. He was just chilled through, and therefore as ready for his own hearth as a long journey could have made him, when a gray thing loped past in the flinty dust, showing him sudden awful eyes and tongue of red fire.

Gaspard clapped the house door to behind him and put up the bar. He was not afraid of Phips and the fleet, of battle or night attack, but the terror which walked in the darkness of sorcerers' times abjectly bowed his old legs.

"O good Ste. Anne, pray for us!" he whispered, using an invocation familiar to his lips. "If loups-garous are abroad, also, what is to become of this unhappy land?"

There was a rattling knock on his door. It might be made by the hilt of a sword; or did a loup-garou ever clatter paw against man's dwelling? Gaspard climbed on his bed.

"Father Gaspard! Father Gaspard! Are you within?"

"Who is there?"

"Le Moyne de Sainte-Hélène. Don't you know my voice?"

"My master Sainte-Hélène, are you alone?"

"Quite alone, except for my horse tied to your apple-tree. Let me in."

The command was not to be slighted. Gaspard got down and admitted his visitor. More than once had Sainte-Hélène come to this hearth. He appreciated the large fire, and sat down on a chair with heavy legs which were joined by bars resting on the floor.

"My hands tingle. The dust on these flint roads is cold."

"But Monsieur Sainte-Hélène never walked with his hands in the dust," protested Gaspard. The erect figure, bright with all the military finery of that period, checked even his superstition by imposing another kind of awe.

"The New England men expect to make us bite it yet," responded Sainte-Hélène. "Saint-Denis is anxious about you, old man. Why don't you go to the fort?"

"I will go to-morrow," promised Gaspard, relaxing sheepishly from terror. "These New Englanders have not yet landed, and one's own bed is very comfortable in the cool nights."

"I am used to sleeping anywhere."

"Yes, monsieur, for you are young."

"It would make you young again, Gaspard, to see Count Frontenac. I wish all New France had seen him yesterday when he defied Phips and sent the envoy back to the fleet. The officer was sweating;

our mischievous fellows had blinded him at the water's edge, and dragged him, to the damage of his shins, over all the barricades of Mountain Street. He took breath and courage when they turned him loose before the governor,—though the sight of Frontenac startled him,—and handed over the letter of his commandant requiring the surrender of Quebec."

"My faith, Monsieur Sainte-Hélène, did the governor blow him out of the room?"

"The man offered his open watch, demanding an answer within the hour. The governor said, 'I do not need so much time. Go back at once to your master and tell him I will answer this insolent message by the mouths of my cannon.'"

"By all the saints, that was a good word!" swore Gaspard, slapping his knee with his wool cap. "Neither the Iroquois nor the Bostonnais will run over us, now that the old governor is back. You heard him say it, monsieur?"

"I heard him, yes; for all his officers

stood by. La Hontan was there, too, and that pet of La Hontan's, Baron de Saint-Castin's half-breed son, of Pentegoet."

The martial note in the officer's voice sunk to contempt. Gaspard was diverted from the governor to recognize, with the speechless perception of an untrained mind, that jealousy which men established in the world have of very young men. The male instinct of predominance is fierce even in saints. Le Moyne de Sainte-Hélène, though of the purest stock in New France, had no prejudice against a half-breed.

"How is Mademoiselle Clementine?" inquired Gaspard, arriving at the question in natural sequence. "You will see her oftener now than when you had to ride from the fort."

The veins looked black in his visitor's face. "Ask the little Saint-Castin. Boys stand under windows and talk to women now. Men have to be reconnoitering the enemy."

"Monsieur Anselm de Saint-Castin is the

son of a good fighter," observed Gaspard. "It is said the New England men hate his very name."

"Anselm de Saint-Castin is barely eighteen years old."

"It is the age of Mademoiselle Clementine."

The old habitant drew his three-legged stool to the hearth corner, and took the liberty of sitting down as the talk was prolonged. He noticed the leaden color which comes of extreme weariness and depression dulling Sainte-Hélène's usually dark and rosy skin. Gaspard had heard that this young man was quickest afoot, readiest with his weapon, most untiring in the dance, and keenest for adventure of all the eight brothers in his noble family. He had done the French arms credit in the expedition to Hudson Bay and many another brush with their enemies. The fire was burning high and clear, lighting rafters and their curious brown tassels of smoked meat, and making the crucifix over the bed shine out the whitest spot in a smoke-stained room.

"Father Gaspard," inquired Sainte-Hélène suddenly, "did you ever hear of such a thing as a loup-garou?"

The old habitant felt terror returning with cold feet up his back and crowding its blackness upon him through the windows. Yet as he rolled his eyes at the questioner he felt piqued at such ignorance of his natural claims.

"Was I not born on the island of Orleans, monsieur?"

Everybody knew that the island of Orleans had been from the time of its discovery the abode of loups-garous, sorcerers, and all those uncanny cattle that run in the twilights of the world. The western point of its wooded ridge, which parts the St. Lawrence for twenty-two miles, from Beauport to Beaupré, lay opposite Gaspard's door.

"Oh, you were born on the island of Orleans?"

"Yes, monsieur," answered Gaspard, with the pride we take in distinction of any kind.

"But you came to live in Beauport parish."

"Does a goat turn to a pig, monsieur, because you carry it to the north shore?"

"Perhaps so: everything changes."

Sainte-Hélène leaned forward, resting his arms on the arms of the chair. He wrinkled his eyelids around central points of fire.

"What is a loup-garou?"

"Does monsieur not know? Monsieur Sainte-Hélène surely knows that a loup-garou is a man-wolf."

"A man-wolf," mused the soldier. "But when a person is so afflicted, is he a man or is he a wolf?"

"It is not an affliction, monsieur; it is sorcery."

"I think you are right. Then the wretched man-wolf is past being prayed for?"

"If one should repent" —

"I don't repent anything," returned Sainte-Hélène; and Gaspard's jaw relaxed, and he had the feeling of pin-feathers in his hair. "Is he a man or is he a wolf?" repeated the questioner.

"The loup-garou is a man, but he takes the form of a wolf."

"Not all the time?"

"No, monsieur, not all the time?"

"Of course not."

Gaspard experienced with us all this paradox: that the older we grow, the more visible becomes the unseen. In childhood the external senses are sharp; but maturity fuses flesh and spirit. He wished for a priest, desiring to feel the arm of the Church around him. It was late October, — a time which might be called the yearly Sabbath of loups-garous.

"And what must a loup-garou do with himself?" pursued Sainte-Hélène. "I should take to the woods, and sit and lick my chaps, and bless my hide that I was for the time no longer a man."

"Saints! monsieur, he goes on a chase. He runs with his tongue lolled out, and his eyes red as blood."

"What color are my eyes, Gaspard?"

The old Frenchman sputtered, "Monsieur, they are very black."

Sainte-Hélène drew his hand across them.

"It must be your firelight that is so red. I have been seeing as through a glass of claret ever since I came in."

Gaspard moved farther into the corner, the stool legs scraping the floor. Though every hair on his body crawled with superstition, he could not suspect Le Moyne de Sainte-Hélène. Yet the familiar face altered strangely while he looked at it: the nose sunk with sudden emaciation, and the jaws lengthened to a gaunt muzzle. There was a crouching forward of the shoulders, as if the man were about to drop on his hands and feet. Gaspard had once fallen down unconscious in haying time; and this recalled to him the breaking up and shimmering apart of a solid landscape. The deep cleft mouth parted, lifting first at the corners and showing teeth, then widening to the utterance of a low howl.

Gaspard tumbled over the stool, and, seizing it by a leg, held it between himself and Sainte-Hélène.

"What is the matter, Gaspard?" exclaimed the officer, clattering his scabbard against the chair as he rose, his lace and plumes and ribbons stirring anew. Many a woman in the province had not as fine and sensitive a face as the one confronting the old habitant.

Gaspard stood back against the wall, holding the stool with its legs bristling towards Sainte-Hélène. He shook from head to foot.

"Have I done anything to frighten you? What is the matter with me, Gaspard, that people should treat me as they do? It is unbearable! I take the hardest work, the most dangerous posts; and they are against me — against me."

The soldier lifted his clenched fists, and turned his back on the old man. The fire showed every curve of his magnificent stature. Wind, diving into the chimney, strove against the sides for freedom, and startled the silence with its hollow rumble.

"I forded the St. Charles when the tide was rising, to take you back with me to the fort. I see you dread the New Englanders less than you do me. She told her father she feared you were ill. But every one is well," said Sainte-Hélène, lowering his arms and making for the door. And it sounded like an accusation against the world.

He was scarcely outside in the wind, though still holding the door, when Gaspard was ready to put up the bar.

"Good-night, old man."

"Good-night, monsieur, good-night, good-night!" called Gaspard, with quavering dispatch. He pushed the door, but Sainte-Hélène looked around its edge. Again the officer's face had changed, pinched by the wind, and his eyes were full of mocking laughter.

"I will say this for a loup-garou, Father Gaspard: a loup-garou may have a harder time in this world than the other beasts, but he is no coward; he can make a good death."

Ashes spun out over the floor, and smoke rolled up around the joists, as Sainte-Hélène shut himself into the darkness. Not satisfied with barring the door, the old habitant pushed his chest against it. To this he added the chair and stool, and barricaded it further with his night's supply of firewood.

"Would I go over the ford of the St. Charles with him?" Gaspard hoarsely whispered as he crossed himself. "If the New England men were burning my house, I would not go. And how can a loup-garou get over that water? The St. Charles is blessed; I am certain it is blessed. Yet he talked about fording it like any Christian."

The old habitant was not clear in his mind what should be done, except that it was no business of his to meddle with one of Frontenac's great officers and a noble of New France. But as a measure of safety for himself he took down his bottle of holy water, hanging on the wall for emergencies, and sprinkled every part of his dwelling.

Next morning, however, when the misty autumn light was on the hills, promising a clear day and penetrating sunshine, as soon as he awoke he felt ashamed of the barricade, and climbed out of bed to remove it.

"The time has at last come when I am obliged to go to the fort," thought Gaspard, groaning. "Governor Frontenac will not permit any sorcery in his presence. The New England men might do me no harm, but I cannot again face a loup-garou."

He dressed himself accordingly, and, taking his gathered coin from its hiding-place, wrapped every piece separately in a bit of rag, slid it into his deep pocket, and sewed the pocket up. Then he cut off enough bacon to toast on the raked-out coals for his breakfast, and hid the rest under the floor. There was no fastening on the outside of Gaspard's house. He was obliged to latch the door, and leave it at the mercy of the enemy.

Nothing was stirring in the frosted world. He could not yet see the citadel clearly, or the heights of Levis; but the ascent to Montmorenci bristled with naked trees, and in the stillness he could hear the roar of the falls. Gaspard ambled along his belt of ground to take a last look. It was like a patchwork quilt: a square of wheat stubble showed here, and a few yards of brown prostrate peavines showed there; his hayfield was less than a stone's throw long; and his garden beds, in triangles and sections of all shapes, filled the interstices of more ambitious crops.

He had nearly reached the limit of the farm, and entered his neck of woods, when the breathing of a cow trying to nip some comfort from the frosty sod delighted his ear. The pretty milker was there, with her calf at her side. Gaspard stroked and patted them. Though the New Englanders should seize them for beef, he could not regret they were wending home again. That invisible cord binding him to his own place, which had wrenched his vitals as it stretched, now drew him back like fate. He worked several hours to make his truants a concealing corral of hay and stakes and straw and stumps at a place where a hill spring threaded across his land, and then returned between his own boundaries to the house again.

The homesick zest of one who has traveled made his lips and unshaven chin protrude, as he smelled the good interior. There was the wooden crane. There was his wife's old wheel. There was the sacred row of children's snow-shoes, which the priest had spared from burning. One really had to leave home to find out what home was.

But a great hubbub was beginning in Phips's fleet. Fifes were screaming, drums were beating, and shouts were lifted and answered by hearty voices. After their long deliberation, the New Englanders had agreed upon some plan of attack. Gaspard went down to his landing, and watched boatload follow boatload, until the river was swarming with little craft pulling directly for Beauport. He looked uneasily toward Quebec. The old lion in the citadel hardly waited for Phips to shift position, but sent the first shot booming out to meet him. The New England cannon answered, and soon Quebec height and Levis palisades rumbled prodigious thunder, and the whole day was black with smoke and streaked with fire.

Gaspard took his gun, and trotted along his farm to the cover of the trees. He had learned to fight in the Indian fashion; and Le Moyne de Sainte-Hélène fought the same way. Before the boatloads of New Englanders had all waded through tidal mud, and ranged themselves by companies on the bank, Sainte-Hélène, who had been dispatched by Frontenac at the first drumbeat on the river, appeared, ready to check them, from the woods of Beauport. He had, besides three hundred sharpshooters, the Lorette Hurons and the muster of Beauport militia, all men with homes to save.

The New Englanders charged them, a solid force, driving the light-footed bush fighters. But it was like driving the wind, which turns, and at some unexpected quarter is always ready for you again.

This long-range fighting went on until nightfall, when the English commander, finding that his tormentors had disappeared as suddenly as they had appeared in the morning, tried to draw his men together at the St. Charles ford, where he expected some small vessels would be sent to help him across. He made a night camp here, without any provisions.

Gaspard's house was dark, like the deserted Beauport homes all that night; yet one watching might have seen smoke issuing from his chimney toward the stars. The weary New England men did not forage through these places, nor seek shelter in them. It was impossible to know where Indians and Frenchmen did not lie in ambush. On the other side of the blankets which muffled Gaspard's windows, however, firelight shone with its usual ruddiness, showing the seignior of Beauport prostrate on his old tenant's bed. Juchereau de Saint-Denis was wounded, and La Hontan, who was with the skirmishers, and Gaspard had brought him in the dark down to the farmhouse as the nearest hospital. Baron La Hontan was skillful in surgery; most men had need to be in those days. He took the keys, and groped into the seigniory house for the linen chest, and provided lint and bandages, and brought cordials from the cellar; making his patient as comfortable as a wounded man who was a veteran in years could be made in the first fever and thirst of suffering. La Hontan knew the woods, and crept away before dawn to a hidden bivouac of Hurons and militia; wiry and venturesome in his age as he had been in his youth. But Saint-Denis lay helpless and partially delirious in Gaspard's house all Thursday, while the bombardment of Quebec made the earth tremble, and the New England ships were being splintered by Frontenac's cannon; while Sainte-Hélène and his brother themselves manned the two batteries of Lower

Town, aiming twenty-four-pound balls directly against the fleet; while they cut the cross of St. George from the flagstaff of the admiral, and Frenchmen above them in the citadel rent the sky with joy; while the fleet, ship by ship, with shattered masts and leaking hulls, drew off from the fight, some of them leaving cable and anchor, and drifting almost in pieces; while the land force, discouraged, sick, and hungry, waited for the promised help which never came.

Thursday night was so cold that the St. Charles was skimmed with ice, and hoarfrost lay white on the fields. But Saint-Denis was in the fire of fever, and Gaspard, slipping like a thief, continually brought him fresh water from the spring.

He lay there on Friday, while the land force, refreshed by half rations sent from the almost wrecked fleet, made a last stand, fighting hotly as they were repulsed from New France. It was twilight on Friday when Sainte-Hélène was carried into Gaspard's house and laid on the floor. Gaspard felt emboldened to take the blankets from a window and roll them up to place under the soldier's head. Many Beauport people were even then returning to their homes. The land force did not reëmbark until the next night, and the invaders did not entirely withdraw for four days; but Quebec was already yielding up its refugees. A disabled foe — though a brave and stubborn one — who had his ships to repair, if he would not sink in them, was no longer to be greatly dreaded.

At first the dusk room was packed with Hurons and Montreal men. This young seignior Sainte-Hélène was one of the best leaders of his time. They were indignant that the enemy's last scattering shots had picked him off. The surgeon and La Hontan put all his followers out of the door, — he was scarcely conscious that they stood by him, — and left, beside his brother Longueuil, only one young man who had helped carry him in.

Saint-Denis, on the bed, saw him with the swimming eyes of fever. The seignior of

Beauport had hoped to have Sainte-Hélène for his son-in-law. His little Clementine, the child of his old age, — it was after all a fortunate thing that she was shut for safety in Quebec, while her father depended for care on Gaspard. Saint-Denis tried to see Sainte-Hélène's face; but the surgeon's helpers constantly balked him, stooping and rising and reaching for things. And presently a face he was not expecting to see grew on the air before him.

Clementine's foot had always made a light click, like a sheep's on a naked floor. But Saint-Denis did not hear her enter. She touched her cheek to her father's. It was smooth and cold from the October air. Clementine's hair hung in large pale ringlets; for she was an ashen maid, gray-toned and subdued; the roughest wind never ruffled her smoothness. She made her father know that she had come with Beauport women and men from Quebec, as soon as any were allowed to leave the fort, to escort her. She leaned against the bed, soft as a fleece, yielding her head to her father's painful fondling. There was no heroism in Clementine; but her snug domestic ways made him happy in his house.

"Sainte-Hélène is wounded," observed Saint-Denis.

She cast a glance of fright over her shoulder.

"Did you not see him when you came in?"

"I saw some one; but it is to you that I have been wishing to come since Wednesday night."

"I shall get well; they tell me it is not so bad with me. But how is it with Sainte-Hélène?"

"I do not know, father."

"Where is young Saint-Castin? Ask him."

"He is helping the surgeon, father."

"Poor child, how she trembles! I would thou hadst stayed in the fort, for these sights are unfit for women. New France can as ill spare him as we can, Clementine. Was that his groan?"

She cowered closer to the bed, and answered, "I do not know."

Saint-Denis tried to sit up in bed, but was obliged to resign himself, with a gasp, to the straw pillows.

Night pressed against the unblinded window. A stir, not made by the wind, was heard at the door, and Frontenac, and Frontenac's Récollet confessor, and Sainte-Hélène's two brothers from the citadel, came into the room. The governor of New France was imposing in presence. Perhaps there was no other officer in the province to whom he would have galloped in such haste from Quebec. It was a tidal moment in his affairs, and Frontenac knew the value of such moments better than most men. But Sainte-Hélène did not know the governor was there. The Récollet father fell on his knees and at once began his office.

Longueuil sat down on Gaspard's stool and covered his face against the wall. He had been hurt by a spent bullet, and one arm needed bandaging, but he said nothing about it, though the surgeon was now at liberty, standing and looking at a patient for whom nothing could be done. The sterner brothers watched, also, silent, as Normans taught themselves to be in trouble. The sons of Charles Le Moyne carried his name and the lilies of France from the Gulf of St. Lawrence to the Gulf of Mexico.

Anselm de Saint-Castin had fought two days alongside the man who lay dying. The boy had an ardent face, like his father's. He was sorry, with the skin-deep commiseration of youth for those who fall, whose falling thins the crowded ranks of competition. But he was not for a moment unconscious of the girl hiding her head against her father from the sight of death. The hope of one man forever springing beside the grave of another must work sadness in God. Yet Sainte-Hélène did not know any young supplanter was there. He did not miss or care for the fickle vanity of applause; he did not torment himself with the spectres of the mind, or feel himself shrinking with the littleness of jealousy; he did not hunger for a love that was not in the world, or waste a Titan's passion on a human ewe any more. For him, the aching and bewilderment, exaltations and self-distrusts, animal gladness and subjection to the elements, were done.

Clementine's father beckoned to the boy, and put her in his care.

"Take her home to the women," Saint-Denis whispered. "She is not used to war and such sight as these. And bid some of the older ones stay with her."

Anselm and Clementine went out, their hands just touching as he led her in wide avoidance of the figure on the floor. Sainte-Hélène did not know the boy and girl left him, for starlight, for silence together, treading the silvered earth in one cadenced step, as he awaited that moment when the solitary spirit finds its utmost loneliness.

Gaspard also went out. When the governor sat in his armchair, and his seignior lay on the bed, and Le Moyne de Sainte-

Hélène was stretched that way on the floor, it could hardly be decent for an old habitant to stand by, even cap in hand. Yet he could scarcely take his eyes from the familiar face as it changed in phosphorescent light. The features lifted themselves with firm nobility, expressing an archangel's beauty. Sainte-Hélène's lips parted, and above the patter of the reciting Récollet the watchers were startled by one note like the sigh of a wind-harp.

The Montreal militia, the Lorette Hurons, and Beauport men were still thronging about, overflowing laterally upon the other farms. They demanded word of the young seignior, hushing their voices. Some of them had gone into Gaspard's milk cave and handed out stale milk for their own and their neighbors' refreshment. A group were sitting on the crisp ground, with a lantern in their midst, playing some game; their heads and shoulders moving with an alacrity objectless to observers, so closely was the light hemmed in.

Gaspard reached his gateway with the certainty of custom. He looked off at both ends of the world. The starlit stretch of road was almost as deserted as when Quebec shut in the inhabitants of Beauport. From the direction of Montmorenci he saw a gray thing come loping down, showing eyes and tongue of red fire. He screamed an old man's scream, pointing to it, and the cry of "Loup-garou!" brought all Beauport men to their feet. The flints clicked. It was a time of alarms. Two shots were fired together, and an under officer sprung across the fence of a neighboring farm to take command of the threatened action.

The camp of sturdy New Englanders on the St. Charles was hid by a swell in the land. At the outcry, those Frenchmen around the lantern parted company, some recoiling backwards, and others scrambling to seize their guns. But one caught up the lantern, and ran to the struggling beast in the road.

Gaspard pushed into the gathering crowd,

and craned himself to see the thing, also. He saw a gaunt dog, searching yet from face to face for some lost idol, and beating the flinty world with a last thump of propitiation.

Frontenac opened the door and stood upon the doorstep. His head almost reached the overhanging straw thatch.

"What is the alarm, my men?"

"Your excellency," the subaltern answered, "it was nothing but a dog. It came down from Montmorenci, and some of the men shot it."

"Le Moyne de Sainte-Hélène," declared Frontenac, lowering his plumed hat, "has just died for New France."

Gaspard stayed out on his river front until he felt half frozen. The old habitant had not been so disturbed and uncomfortable since his family died of smallpox. Phips's vessels lay near the point of Orleans Island, a few portholes lighting their mass of gloom, while two red lanterns aloft burned like baleful eyes at the lost coast of Canada. Nothing else showed on the river. The distant wall of Levis palisades could be discerned, and Quebec stood a mighty crown, its gems all sparkling. Behind Gaspard, Beauport was alive. The siege was virtually over, and he had not set foot off his farm during Phips's invasion of New France. He did not mind sleeping on the floor, with his heels to the fire. But there were displacements and changes and sorrows which he did mind.

"However," muttered the old man, and it was some comfort to the vague aching in his breast to formulate one fact as solid as the heights around, "it is certain that there are loups-garous."

THE MILL AT PETIT CAP.

August night air, sweet with a half salt breath from the St. Lawrence, met the miller of San Joachim as he looked out; but he bolted the single thick door of the mill, and cast across it into a staple a hook as long as his body and as thick as his arm. At any alarm in the village he must undo these fastenings, and receive the refugees from Montgomery; yet he could not sleep without locking the door. So all that summer he had slept on a bench in the mill basement, to be ready for the call.

All the parishes on the island of Orleans, and on each side of the river, quite to Montmorenci Falls, where Wolfe's army was encamped, had been sacked by that evil man, Captain Alexander Montgomery, whom the English general himself could hardly restrain. San Joachim du Petit Cap need not hope to escape. It was really Wolfe's policy to harry the country which in that despairing summer of 1759 he saw no chance of conquering.

The mill was grinding with a shuddering noise which covered all country night sounds. But so accustomed was the miller to this lullaby that he fell asleep on his chaff cushion directly, without his usual review of the trouble betwixt La Vigne and himself. He was sensitive to his neighbors' claims, and the state of the country troubled him, but he knew he could endure La Vigne's misfortunes better than any other man's.

Loopholes in the hoary stone walls of the basement were carefully covered, but a burning dip on the hearth betrayed them within. There was a deep blackened oven built at right angles to the fireplace in the south wall. The stairway rose like a giant's ladder to the vast dimness overhead. No other such fortress-mill was to be found between Cap Tourmente and the citadel, or indeed anywhere on the St. Lawrence. It had been built not many years before by the Seminaire priests of Quebec for the protection and nourishment of their seigniory, that huge grant of rich land stretching from Beaupré to Cap Tourmente, bequeathed to the church by the first bishop of Canada.

The miller suddenly dashed up with a shout. He heard his wife scream above the rattle of the mill, and stumbling over basement litter he unstopped a loophole and saw the village already mounting in flames.

The mill door's iron-clamped timbers were beaten by a crowd of entreating hands, and he tore back the fastenings and dragged his neighbors in. Children, women, men, fell past him on the basement floor, and he screamed for help to hold the door against Montgomery's men. The priest was the last one to enter and the first to set a shoulder with the miller's. A discharge of firearms from without made lightning in the dim inclosure, and the curé, Father Robineau de Portneuf, reminded his flock of the guns they had stored in the mill basement.

Loopholes were soon manned, and the enemy were driven back from the mill door. The roaring torch of each cottage thatch showed them in the redness of their uniforms, — good marks for enraged refugees; so they drew a little farther westward still, along the hot narrow street of San Joachim du Petit Cap.

At an unoccupied loophole Father Robineau watched his chapel burning, with its meagre enrichments, added year by year. But this was nothing, when his eye dropped to the two or three figures lying face downward on the road. He turned himself toward the wailing of a widow and a mother.

The miller's wife was coming downstairs with a candle, leaving her children huddled in darkness at the top. Those two dozen or more people whom she could see lifting dazed looks at her were perhaps of small account in the province; but they were her friends and neighbors, and bounded her whole experience of the world, except that anxiety of having her son Laurent with

Montcalm's militia. The dip light dropped tallow down her petticoat, and even unheeded on one bare foot.

"My children," exhorted Father Robineau through the wailing of bereaved women, "have patience." The miller's wife stooped and passed a hand across a bright head leaning against the stair side.

"Thy mother is safe, Angèle?"

"Oh, yes, Madame Sandeau."

"Thy father and the children are safe?"

"Oh, yes," testified the miller, passing towards the fireplace, "La Vigne and all his are within. I counted them."

"The saints be praised," said his wife.

"Yes, La Vigne got in safely," added the miller, "while that excellent Jules Martin, our good neighbor, lies scalped out there in the road."[1]

"He does not know what he is saying, Angèle," whispered his wife to the weeping girl. But the miller snatched the candle

---

[1] Wolfe forbade such barbarities, but Montgomery did not always obey. It was practiced on both sides.

from the hearth as if he meant to fling his indignation with it at La Vigne. His worthy act, however, was to light the sticks he kept built in the fireplace for such emergency. A flame arose, gradually revealing the black earthen floor, the swarm of refugees, and even the tear-suspending lashes of little children's eyes.

La Vigne appeared, sitting with his hands in his hair. And the miller's wife saw there was a strange young demoiselle among the women of the côte, trying to quiet them. She had a calm dark beauty and an elegance of manner unusual to the provinces, and even Father Robineau beheld her with surprise.

"Mademoiselle, it is unfortunate that you should be in Petit Cap at this time," said the priest.

"Father, I count myself fortunate," she answered, "if no worse calamity has befallen me. My father is safe within here. Can you tell me anything about my husband, Captain De Mattissart, of the Languedoc regiment, with General Montcalm?"

"Madame, I never saw your husband."

"He was to meet me with escort at Petit Cap. We landed on a little point, secretly, with no people at all, and my father would have returned in his sailboat, but my husband did not meet us. These English must have cut him off, father."

"These are not times in which a woman should stir abroad," said the priest.

"Monsieur the curé, there is no such comfortable doctrine for a man with a daughter," said a figure at the nearest loophole, turning and revealing himself by face and presence a gentilhomme. "Especially a daughter married to a soldier. I am Denys of Bonaventure, galloping hither out of Acadia at her word of command."

The priest made him a gesture of respect and welcome.

"One of the best men in Acadia should be of advantage to us here. But I regret madame's exposure. You were not by yourselves attempting to reach Montcalm's camp?"

"How do I know, monsieur the curé? My daughter commanded this expedition." Denys of Bonaventure shrugged his shoulders and spread his palms with a smile.

"We were going to knock at the door of the curé of Petit Cap," said the lady. "There was nothing else for us to do; but the English appeared."

Successive shots at the loopholes proved that the English had not yet disappeared. Denys seized his gun again, and turned to the defense, urging that the children and women be sent out of the way of balls.

Father Robineau, on his part, gave instant command to the miller's wife, and she climbed the stairs again, heading a long line of distressed neighbors.

The burrs were in the second story, and here the roaring of the mill took possession of all the shuddering air. Every massive joist half growing from dimness overhead was hung with ghostly shreds of cobweb; and on the grayish whiteness of the floor the children's naked soles cut out oblongs dotted with toe-marks.

Mother Sandeau made her way first to an inclosed corner, and looked around to invite the attention of her followers. Such violence had been done to her stolid habits that she seemed to need the sight of her milk-room to restore her to intelligent action. The group was left in half darkness while she thrust her candle into the milk-room, showing its orderly array of flowered bowls amidst moist coolness. Here was a promise of sustenance to people dependent for the next mouthful of food. "It will last a few days, even if the cows be driven off and killed!" said the miller's good wife.

But there was the Acadian lady to be first thought of. Neighbors could be easily spread out on the great floor, with rolls of bedding. Her own oasis of homestead stood open, showing a small fireplace hollowed in one wall, two feet above the floor; table and heavy chairs; and sleeping rooms beyond. Yet none of these things were good enough to offer such a stranger.

"Take no thought about me, good friend,"

said the girl, noticing Mother Sandeau's anxiously creased face. "I shall presently go back to my father."

"But, no," exclaimed the miller's wife, "the priest forbids women below, and there is my son's bridal room upstairs with even a dressing-table in it. I only held back on account of Angèle La Vigne," she added to comprehending neighbors, "but Angèle will attend to the lady there."

"Angèle will gladly attend to the lady anywhere," spoke out Angèle's mother, with a resentment of her child's position which ruin could not crush. "It is the same as if marriage was never talked of between your son Laurent and her."

"Yes, neighbor, yes," said the miller's wife appeasingly. It was not her fault that a pig had stopped the marriage. She gave her own candle to Angèle, with a motherly look. The girl had a pink and golden prettiness unusual among habitantes. Though all flush was gone out of her skin under the stress of the hour, she retained the innocent clear pallor of an infant. Angèle hurried to straighten her disordered dress before taking the candle, and then led Madame De Mattissart up the next flight of stairs.

The mill's noise had forced talkers to lift their voices, and it now half dulled the clamp of habitante shoes below, and the whining of children longing again for sleep. Huge square wooden hoppers were shaking down grain, and the two or three square sashes in the thickness of front wall let in some light from the burning côte.

The building's mighty stone hollows were as cool as the dew-pearled and river-vapored landscape outside. Occasional shots from below kept reverberating upward through two more floors overhead.

Laurent's bridal apartment was of new boards built like a deck cabin at one side of the third story. It was hard for Angèle to throw open the door of this sacred little place which she had expected to enter as a bride, and the French officer's young wife understood it, restraining the girl's hand.

"Stop, my child. Let us not go in. I came up here simply to quiet the others."

"But you were to rest in this chamber, madame."

"Do you think I can rest when I do not know whether I am wife or widow?"

The young girls looked at each other with piteous eyes.

"This is a terrible time, madame."

"It will, however, pass by, in some fashion."

"But what shall I do for you, madame? Where will you sit? Is there nothing you require?"

"Yes, I am thirsty. Is there not running water somewhere in this mill?"

"There is the flume-chamber overhead," said Angèle. "I will set the light here, and go down for a cup, madame."

"Do not. We will go to the flume-chamber together. My hands, my throat, my eyes burn. Go on, Angèle, show me the way."

Laurent's room, therefore, was left in

darkness, holding unseen its best furniture, the family's holiday clothes of huge grained flannel, and the little yellow spinning-wheel, with its pile of unspun wool like forgotten snow.

In the fourth story, as below, deep-set swinging windows had small square panes, well dusted with flour. Nothing broke the monotony of wall except a row of family snow-shoes. The flume-chamber, inclosed from floor to ceiling, suggested a grain's sprouting here and there in its upright humid boards.

As the two girls glanced around this grim space, they were startled by silence through the building, for the burrs ceased to work. Feet and voices indeed stirred below, but the sashes no longer rattled. Then a tramping seemed following them up, and Angèle dragged the young lady behind a stone pillar, and blew out their candle.

"What are you doing?" demanded Madame De Mattissart in displeasure. "If the door has been forced, should we desert our fathers?"

"It is not that," whispered Angèle. And before she could give any reason for her impulse, the miller's head and light appeared above the stairs. It was natural enough for Angèle La Vigne to avoid Laurent's father. What puzzled her was to see her own barefooted father creeping after the miller, his red wool night-cap pulled over dejected brows.

These good men had been unable to meet without quarreling since the match between Laurent and Angèle was broken off, on account of a pig which Father La Vigne would not add to her dower. Angèle had a blanket, three dishes, six tin plates, and a kneading-trough; at the pig her father drew the line, and for a pig Laurent's father contended. But now all the La Vigne pigs were roasted or scattered, Angèle's dower was destroyed, and what had a ruined habitant to say to the miller of Petit Cap?

Father Robineau had stopped the mill because its noise might cover attacks. As the miller ungeared his primitive machinery, he had thought of saving water in the flume-chamber. There were wires and chains for shutting off its escape.

He now opened a door in the humid wall and put his candle over the clear, dark water. The flume no longer furnished a supply, and he stared open-lipped, wondering if the enemy had meddled with his water-gate in the upland.

The flume, at that time the most ambitious wooden channel on the north shore, supported on high stilts of timber, dripped all the way from a hill stream to the fourth story of Petit Cap mill. The miller had watched it escape burning thatches, yet something had happened at the dam. Shreds of moss, half floating and half moored, reminded him to close the reservoir, and he had just moved the chains when La Vigne startled him by speaking at his ear.

The miller recoiled, but almost in the action his face recovered itself. He wore a gray wool night-cap, and its tassel hung down over one lifted eyebrow.

"Pierre Sandeau, my friend," opened La

Vigne with a whimper, "I followed you up here to weep with you."

"You did well," replied the miller bluntly, "for I am a ruined man with the parish to feed, unless the Seminaire fathers take pity on me."

"Yes, you have lost more than all of us," said La Vigne.

"I am not the man to measure losses and exult over my neighbors," declared the miller; "but how many pigs would you give to your girl's dower now, Guillaume?"

"None at all, my poor Pierre. At least she is not a widow."

"Nor ever likely to be now, since she has no dower to make her a wife."

"How could she be a wife without a husband? Taunt me no more about that pig. I tell you it is worse with you: you have no son."

"What do you mean? I have half a dozen."

"But Laurent is shot."

"Laurent — shot?" whispered the miller, relaxing his flabby face, and letting the candle sink downward until it spread their shadows on the floor.

"Yes, my friend," whimpered La Vigne. "I saw him through my window when the alarm was given. He was doubtless coming to save us all, for an officer was with him. Jules Martin's thatch was just fired. It was bright as sunrise against the hill, and the English saw our Laurent and his officer, no doubt, for they shot them down, and I saw it through my back window."

The miller sunk to his knees, and set the candle on the floor; La Vigne approached and mingled night-cap tassels and groans with him.

"Oh, my son! And I quarreled with thee, Guillaume, about a pig, and made the children unhappy."

"But I was to blame for that, Pierre," wept La Vigne, "and now we have neither pig nor son!"

"Perhaps Montgomery's men have scalped him;" the miller pulled the night-cap from his own head and threw it on the floor in helpless wretchedness.

La Vigne uttered a low bellow in response, and they fell upon each other's necks and were about to lament together in true Latin fashion, when the wife of Montcalm's officer called to them.

She stood out from the shadow of the stone column, dead to all appearances, yet animate, and trying to hold up Angèle whose whole body lapsed downward in half unconsciousness. "Bring water," demanded Madame De Mattissart.

And seeing who had overheard the dreadful news, La Vigne ran to the flume-chamber, and the miller scrambled up and reached over him to dip the first handful. Both stooped within the door, both recoiled, and both raised a yell which echoed among high rafters in the attic above. The miller thought Montgomery's entire troop were stealing into the mill through the flume; for a man's legs protruded from the opening and wriggled with such vigor that his body instantly followed and he dropped into the water.

His beholders seized and dragged him out upon the floor; but he threw off their hands, sprang astride of the door-sill, and stretched himself to the flume mouth to help another man out of it.

La Vigne ran downstairs shrieking for the priest, as if he had seen witchcraft. But the miller stood still, with the candle flaring on the floor behind him, not sure of his son Laurent in militia uniform, but trembling with some hope.

It was Madame De Mattissart's cry to her husband which confirmed the miller's senses. She knew the young officer through the drenching and raggedness of his white and gold uniform; she understood how two wounded men could creep through any length of flume, from which a miller's son would know how to turn off the water. She had no need to ask what their sensations were, sliding down that slimy duct, or how they entered it without being seen by the enemy. Let villagers talk over such matters, and shout and exclaim when they came to hear this strange thing. It was enough that her husband had met her through every danger, and that he was able to stand and receive her in his arms.

Laurent's wound was serious. After all his exertions he fainted; but Angèle took his head upon her knee, and the fathers and mothers and neighbors swarmed around him, and Father Robineau did him doctor's service. Every priest then on the St. Lawrence knew how to dress wounds as well as bind up spirits.

Denys of Bonaventure, notwithstanding the excitement overhead, kept men at the basement loopholes until Montgomery had long withdrawn and returned to camp.

He then felt that he could indulge himself with a sight of his son-in-law, and tiptoed up past the colony of women and children whom the priest had just driven again to their rest on the second floor; past that sacred chamber on the third floor, and on up to the flume loft. There Monsieur De Bonaventure paused, with his head just above the boards, like a pleasant-faced sphinx.

"Accept my salutations, Captain De Mattissart," he said laughing. "I am told that you and this young militia-man floated down the mill-stream into this mill, with the French flag waving over your heads, to the no small discouragement of the English. Quebec will never be taken, monsieur."

Long ago those who found shelter in the mill dispersed to rebuild their homes under a new order of things, or wedded like Laurent and Angèle, and lived their lives and died. Yet, witnessing to all these things, the old mill stands to-day at Petit Cap, huge and cavernous; with its oasis of home, its milk-room, its square hoppers and flume-chamber unchanged. Daylight refuses to follow you into the blackened basement; and the shouts of Montgomery's sacking horde seem to linger in the mighty hollows overhead.

WOLFE'S COVE.

The cannon was for the time silent, the gunners being elsewhere, but a boy's voice called from the bastion: —

"Come out here, mademoiselle. I have an apple for you."

"Where did you get an apple?" replied a girl's voice.

"Monsieur Bigot gave it to me. He has everything the king's stores will buy. His slave was carrying a basketful."

"I do not like Monsieur Bigot. His face is blotched, and he kisses little girls."

"His apples are better than his manners," observed the boy, waiting, knife in hand, for her to come and see that the division was a fair one.

She tiptoed out from the gallery of the commandant's house, the wind blowing her curls back from her shoulders. A bastion of Fort St. Louis was like a balcony in the clouds. The child's lithe, long body made a graceful line in every posture, and her face was vivid with light and expression.

"Perhaps your sick mother would like this apple, Monsieur Jacques. We do not have any in the fort."

The boy flushed. He held the halves ready on his palm.

"I thought of her; but the surgeon might forbid it, and she is not fond of apples when she is well. And you are always fond of apples, Mademoiselle Anglaise."

"My name is Clara Baker. If you call me Mademoiselle Anglaise, I will box your ears."

"But you are English," persisted the boy. "You cannot help it. I am sorry for it myself; and when I am grown I will whip anybody that reproaches you for it."

They began to eat the halves of the apple, forgetful of Jacques's sick mother, and to quarrel as their two nations have done since France and England stood on the waters.

"Don't distress yourself, Monsieur Jacques Repentigny. The English will be the fashion in Quebec when you are grown."

It was amusing to hear her talk his language glibly while she prophesied.

"Do you think your ugly General Wolfe can ever make himself the fashion?" retorted Jacques. "I saw him once across the Montmorenci when I was in my father's camp. His face runs to a point in the middle, and his legs are like stilts."

"His stilts will lift him into Quebec yet."

The boy shook his black queue. He had a cheek in which the flush came and went, and black sparkling eyes.

"The English never can take this province. What can you know about it? You were only a little baby when Madame Ramesay bought you from the Iroquois Indians who had stolen you. If your name had not been on your arm, you would not even know that. But a Le Moyne of Montreal knows all about the province. My grandfather, Le Moyne de Longueuil, was wounded down there at Beauport, when the English came to take Canada before. And his brother Jacques that I am named for — Le Moyne de Sainte-Hélène — was killed. I have often seen the place where he died when I went with my father to our camp."

The little girl pushed back her sleeve, as she did many times a day, and looked at the name tattooed in pale blue upon her arm. Jacques envied her that mark, and she was proud of it. Her traditions were all French, but the indelible stamp, perhaps of an English seaman, reminded her what blood was in her veins.

The children stepped nearer the parapet, where they could see all Quebec Basin, and the French camp stretching its city of tents across the valley of the St. Charles. Beneath them was Lower Town, a huddle of blackened shells and tottering walls.

"See there what the English have done," said Clara, pointing down the sheer rock. "It will be a long time before you and I go down Breakneck Stairs again to see the pretty images in the church of Our Lady of Victories."

"They did that two months ago," replied Jacques. "It was all they could do. And now they are sick of bombarding, and are going home. All their soldiers at Montmorenci and on the point of Orleans are embarking. Their vessels keep running around like hens in a shower, hardly knowing what to do."

"Look at them getting in a line yonder," insisted his born enemy.

"General Montcalm is in front of them at Beauport," responded Jacques.

The ground was moist underfoot, and the rock on which they leaned felt damp. Quebec grayness infused with light softened the autumn world. No one could behold without a leap of the heart that vast reach of river and islands, and palisade and valley, and far-away melting mountain lines. Inside Quebec walls the children could see the Ursuline convent near the top of the slope, showing holes in its roof. Nearly every building in the city had suffered.

Drums began to beat on the British ships ranged in front of Beauport, and a cannon flashed. Its roar was shaken from height to height. Then whole broadsides of fire broke forth, and the earth rumbled with the sound, and scarlet uniforms filled the boats like floating poppies.

"The English may be going home," exulted Clara, "but you now see for yourself, Monsieur Jacques Repentigny, what they intend to do before they go."

"I wish my father had not been sent with his men back to Montreal!" exclaimed Jacques in excitement. "But I shall go down to the camps, anyhow."

"Your mother will cry," threatened the girl.

"My mother is used to war. She often lets me sleep in my father's tent. Tell her I have gone to the camps."

"They will put you in the guard-house."

"They do not put a Repentigny in the guard-house."

"If you will stay here," called the girl,

running after him towards the fortress gate, "I will play anything you wish. The cannon balls might hit you."

Deaf to the threat of danger, he made off through cross-cuts toward the Palace Gate, the one nearest the bridge of boats on the St. Charles River.

"Very good, monsieur. I'll tell your mother," she said, trembling and putting up a lip.

But nothing except noise was attempted at Beauport. Jacques was so weary, as he toiled back uphill in diminishing light, that he gratefully crawled upon a cart and lay still, letting it take him wherever the carter might be going. There were not enough horses and oxen in Canada to move the supplies for the army from Montreal to Quebec by land. Transports had to slip down the St. Lawrence by night, running a gauntlet of vigilant English vessels. Yet whenever the intendant Bigot wanted to shift anything, he did not lack oxen or wheels. Jacques did not talk to the carter, but he knew a load of king's provisions was going out to some favorite of the intendant's who had been set to guard the northern heights. The stealings of this popular civil officer were common talk in Quebec.

That long slope called the Plains of Abraham, which swept away from the summit of the rock toward Cap Rouge, seemed very near the sky. Jacques watched dusk envelop this place. Patches of faded herbage and stripped corn, and a few trees only, broke the monotony of its extent. On the north side, overhanging the winding valley of the St. Charles, the rock's great shoulder was called Côte Ste. Geneviève. The bald plain was about a mile wide, but the cart jogged a mile and a half from Quebec before it reached the tents where its freight was to be discharged.

Habit had taken the young Repentigny daily to his father's camp, but this was the first time he had seen the guard along the heights. Montcalm's soldiers knew him. He was permitted to handle arms. Many a boy of fifteen was then in the ranks, and children of his age were growing used to war. His father called it his apprenticeship to the trade. A few empty houses stood some distance back of the tents; and farther along the precipice, beyond brush and trees, other guards were posted. Seventy men and four cannon completed the defensive line which Montcalm had drawn around the top of the rock. Half the number could have kept it, by vigilance. And it was evident that the officer in charge thought so, and was taking advantage of his general's bounty.

"Remember I am sending you to my field as well as to your own," the boy overheard him say. Nearly all his company were gathered in a little mob before his tent. He sat there on a camp stool. They were Canadians from Lorette, anxious for leave of absence, and full of promises.

"Yes, monsieur, we will remember your field." "Yes, Captain Vergor, your grain as soon as we have gathered ours in." "It shall be done, captain."

Jacques had heard of Vergor. A few years before, Vergor had been put under arrest for giving up Fort Beauséjour, in Acadia, to the English without firing a shot. The boy thought it strange that such a man should be put in charge of any part of the defensive cordon around Quebec. But Vergor had a friend in the intendant Bigot, who knew how to reinstate his disgraced favorites. The arriving cart drew the captain's attention from his departing men. He smiled, his depressed nose and fleshy lips being entirely good-natured.

"A load of provisions, and a recruit for my company," he said.

"Monsieur the captain needs recruits," observed Jacques.

"Society is what I need most," said Vergor. "And from appearances I am going to have it at my supper which the cook is about to set before me."

"I think I will stay all night here," said Jacques.

"You overwhelm me," responded Vergor.

"There are so many empty tents."

"Fill as many of them as you can," suggested Vergor. "You are doubtless much away from your mother, inspecting the troops; but what will madame say if you fail to answer at her roll call to-night?"

"Nothing. I should be in my father's tent at Montreal, if she had been able to go when he was ordered back there."

"Who is your father?"

"Le Gardeur de Repentigny."

Vergor drew his lips together for a soft whistle, as he rose to direct the storing of his goods.

"It is a young general with whom I am to have the honor of messing. I thought he had the air of camps and courts the moment I saw his head over the side of the cart."

Many a boy secretly despises the man to whose merry insolence he submits. But the young Repentigny felt for Vergor such contempt as only an incompetent officer inspires.

No sentinels were stationed. The few

soldiers remaining busied themselves over their mess fires. Jacques looked down a cove not quite as steep as the rest of the cliff, yet as nearly perpendicular as any surface on which trees and bushes can take hold. It was clothed with a thick growth of sere weeds, cut by one hint of a diagonal line. Perhaps laborers at a fulling mill now rotting below had once climbed this rock. Rain had carried the earth from above in small cataracts down its face, making a thin alluvial coating. A strip of land separated the rock from the St. Lawrence, which looked wide and gray in the evening light. Showers raked the far-off opposite hills. Leaves showing scarlet or orange were dulled by flying mist.

The boy noticed more boats drifting up river on the tide than he had counted in Quebec Basin.

"Where are all the vessels going?" he asked the nearest soldier.

"Nowhere. They only move back and forth with the tide."

"But they are English ships. Why don't you fire on them?"

"We have no orders. And besides, our own transports have to slip down among them at night. One is pretty careful not to knock the bottom out of the dish which carries his meat."

"The English might land down there some dark night."

"They may land; but, unfortunately for themselves, they have no wings."

The boy did not answer, but he thought, "If my father and General Levis were posted here, wings would be of no use to the English."

His distinct little figure, outlined against the sky, could be seen from the prisoners' ship. One prisoner saw him without taking any note that he was a child. Her eyes were fierce and red-rimmed. She was the only woman on the deck, having come up the gangway to get rid of habitantes. These fellow-prisoners of hers were that moment putting their heads together below and talking about Mademoiselle Jeannette Descheneaux. They were perhaps the only people in the world who took any thought of her. Highlanders and seamen moving on deck scarcely saw her. In every age of the world beauty has ruled men. Jeannette Descheneaux was a big, manly Frenchwoman, with a heavy voice. In Quebec, she was a contrast to the exquisite and diaphanous creatures who sometimes kneeled beside her in the cathedral, or looked out of sledge or sedan chair at her as she tramped the narrow streets. They were the beauties of the governor's court, who permitted in a new land the corrupt gallantries of Versailles. She was the daughter of a shoemaker, and had been raised to a semi-official position by the promotion of her brother in the government. Her brother had grown rich with the company of speculators who preyed on the province and the king's stores. He had one motherless child, and Jeannette took charge of it and his house until the child died. She was perhaps a masculine nourisher of infancy; yet the upright mark between her black eyebrows, so deep that it seemed made by a hatchet, had never been there before the baby's death; and it was by stubbornly venturing too far among the parishes to seek the child's foster mother, who was said to be in some peril at Petit Cap, that Jeannette got herself taken prisoner.

For a month this active woman had been a dreamer of dreams. Every day the prison ship floated down to Quebec, and her past stood before her like a picture. Every night it floated up to Cap Rouge, where French camp fires flecked the gorge and the north shore stretching westward. No strict guard was kept over the prisoners. She sat on the ship's deck, and a delicious languor, unlike any former experience, grew and grew upon her. The coaxing graces of pretty women she never caricatured. Her skin was of the dark red tint which denotes a testy disposition. She had fierce one-sided wars for trivial reasons, and was by nature an aggressive partisan, even in the cause of a dog or a cat. Being a woman of few phrases, she repeated these as often as she had occasion for speech, and divided the world simply into two classes: two or three individuals, including herself, were human beings; the rest of mankind she denounced, in a voice which shook the walls, as spawn. One does not like to be called spawn.

Though Jeannette had never given herself to exaggerated worship, she was religious. The lack of priest and mass on the prison transport was blamed for the change which came over her. A haze of real feminine softness, like the autumn's purpling of rocks, made her bones less prominent. But the habitantes, common women from the parishes, who had children and a few of their men with them, saw what ailed her. They noticed that while her enmity to the English remained unchanged, she would not hear a word against the Highlanders, though Colonel Fraser and his Seventy-Eighth Highland regiment had taken her prisoner.

It is true, Jeannette was treated with deference, and her food was sent to her from the officer's table, and she had privacy on the ship which the commoner prisoners had not. It is also true that Colonel Fraser was a gentleman, detesting the parish-burning to which his command was ordered for a time. But the habitantes laid much to his blue eyes and yellow hair, and the picturesqueness of the red and pale green Fraser tartan. They nudged one another when Jeannette began to plait her strong black locks, and make a coronet of them on her sloping head. She was always exact and neat in her dress, and its mannishness stood her in good stead during her month's imprisonment. Rough wool was her invariable wear, instead of taffetas and silky furs, which Quebec women delighted in. She groomed herself carefully each day for that approach to the English camp at Point Levi which the tide accomplished. Her features could be distinguished half a mile. On the days when Colonel Fraser's fezlike plumed bonnet was lifted to her in the camp, she went up the river again in a trance of quiet. On other days the habitantes laughed, and said to one another, "Mademoiselle will certainly break through the deck with her tramping."

There was a general restlessness on the prison ship. The English sailors wanted to go home. The Canadians had been patient since the middle of August. But this particular September night, as they drifted up past the rock, and saw the defenses of their country bristling against them, the feeling of homesickness vented itself in complaints. Jeannette was in her cabin, and heard them abuse Colonel Fraser and his Highlanders as kidnapers of women and children, and burners of churches. She came out of her retreat, and hovered over them like a hawk. The men pulled their caps off, drolly grinning.

"It is true," added one of them, "that General Montcalm is to blame for letting the parishes burn. And at least he might take us away from the English."

"Do you think Monsieur de Montcalm has nothing to do but bring you in off the river?" demanded Jeannette.

"Mademoiselle does not want to be brought in," retorted one of the women. "As for us, we are not in love with these officers who wear petticoats, or with any of our enemies."

"Spawn!" Jeanette hurled at them. Yet her partisan fury died in her throat. She went up on deck to be away from her accusers. The seamed precipice, the indented cove with the child's figure standing at the top, and all the panorama to which she was so accustomed by morning light or twilight passed before her without being seen by her fierce red-rimmed eyes.

Jeannette Descheneaux had walked through the midst of colonial intrigues without knowing that they existed. Men she ignored; and she could not now account for her keen knowledge that there was a colonel of the Seventy-Eighth Highlanders. Her entanglement had taken her in the very simplicity of childhood. She could not blame him. He had done nothing but lift his bonnet to her, and treat her with deference because he was sorry she had fallen into his hands. But at first she fought with silent fury the power he unconsciously held over her. She felt only the shame of it, which the habitantes had cast upon her. Nobody had ever called Jeannette Descheneaux a silly woman. In early life it was thought she had a vocation for the convent; but she drew back from that, and now she was suddenly desolate. Her brother had his consolations. There was nothing for her.

Scant tears, oozing like blood, moistened her eyes. She took hold of her throat to strangle a sob. Her teeth chattered in the wind blowing down river. Constellations came up over the rock's long shoulder. Though it was a dark night, the stars were clear. She took no heed of the French camp fires in the gorge and along the bank. The French commander there had followed the erratic motions of English boats until they ceased to alarm him. It was flood tide. The prison ship sat on the water, scarcely swinging.

At one o'clock Jeannette was still on deck, having watched through the midnight of her experience. She had no phrases for her thoughts. They were dumb, but they filled her to the outermost layer of her skin, and deadened sensation.

Boats began to disturb her, however. They trailed past the ship with a muffled swish, all of them disappearing in the darkness. This gathering must have been going on some time before she noticed it. The lantern hanging aloft made a mere warning spot in the darkness, for the lights on deck had been put out. All the English ships, when she looked about her, were to be guessed at, for not a port-hole cast its cylinder of radiance on the water. Night muffled their hulls, and their safety lights hung in a scattered constellation. In one place two lanterns hung on one mast.

Jeannette felt the pull of the ebbing tide.

The ship gave way to it. As it swung, and the monotonous flow of the water became constant, she heard a boat grate, and directly Colonel Fraser came up the vessel's side, and stood on deck where she could touch him. He did not know that the lump of blackness almost beneath his hand was a breathing woman; and if he had known, he would have disregarded her then. But she knew him, from indistinct cap and the white pouch at his girdle to the flat Highland shoes.

Whether the Highlanders on the ship were watching for him to appear as their signal, or he had some private admonition for them, they started up from spots which Jeannette had thought vacant darkness, probably armed and wrapped in their plaids. She did not know what he said to them. One by one they got quickly over the ship's side. She did not form any resolution, and neither did she hesitate; but, drawing tight around her the plaidlike length of shawl which had served her nearly a lifetime, she stood up ready to take her turn.

Jeannette seemed to swallow her heart as she climbed over the rail. The Highlanders were all in the boat except their colonel. He drew in his breath with a startled sound, and she knew the sweep of her skirt must have betrayed her. She expected to fall into the river; but her hand took sure hold of a ladder of rope, and, creeping down backward, she set her foot in the bateau. It was a large and steady open boat. Some of the men were standing. She had entered the bow, and as Colonel Fraser dropped in they cast off, and she sat down, finding a bench as she had found foothold. The Highland officer was beside her. They could not see each other's faces. She was not sure he had detected her. The hardihood which had taken her beyond the French lines in search of one whom she felt under her protection was no longer in her. A cowering woman with a boatload of English soldiers palpitated under the darkness. It was necessary only to steer; both tide and current carried them steadily down.

On the surface of the river, lines of dark objects followed. A fleet of the enemy's transports was moving towards Quebec.

To most women country means home. Jeannette was tenaciously fond of the gray old city of Quebec, but home to her was to be near that Highland officer. Her humiliation passed into the very agony of tenderness. To go wherever he was going was enough. She did not want him to speak to her, or touch her, or give any sign that he knew she was in the world. She wanted to sit still by his side under the negation of darkness and be satisfied. Jeannette had never dreamed how long the hours between turn of tide and dawn may be. They were the principal part of her life.

Keen stars held the sky at immeasurable heights. There was no mist. The chill wind had swept the river clear like a great path. Within reach of Jeannette's hand, but hidden from her, as most of us are hidden from one another, sat one more solitary than herself. He had not her robust body. Disease and anxiety had worn him away while he was hopelessly besieging Quebec. In that last hour before the 13th of September dawned, General Wolfe was groping down river toward one of the most desperate military attempts in the history of the world.

There was no sound but the rustle of the water, the stir of a foot as some standing man shifted his weight, and the light click of metal as guns in unsteady hands touched barrels. A voice, modulating rhythm which Jeannette could not understand, began to speak. General Wolfe was reciting an English poem. The strain upon his soul was more than he could bear, and he relieved it by those low-uttered rhymes. Jeannette did not know one word of English. The meaning which reached her was a dirge, but a noble dirge; the death hymn of a human being who has lived up to his capacities. She felt strangely influenced, as by the neighborhood of some large angel, and at the same time the tragedy of being alive overswept her. For one's duty is never all done; or when we have accomplished it with painstaking care, we are smitten through with finding that the greater things have passed us by.

The tide carried the boats near the great wall of rock. Woods made denser shade on the background of night. The cautious murmur of the speaker was cut short.

"Who goes there?" came the sharp challenge of a French sentry.

The soldiers were silent as dead men.

"France!" answered Colonel Fraser in the same language.

"Of what regiment?"

"The Queen's."

The sentry was satisfied. To the Queen's regiment, stationed at Cap Rouge, belonged the duty of convoying provisions down to Quebec. He did not further peril what he believed to be a French transport by asking for the password.

Jeannette breathed. So low had she

sunk that she would have used her language herself to get the Highland colonel past danger.

It was fortunate for his general that he had the accent and readiness of a Frenchman. Again they were challenged. They could see another sentry running parallel with their course.

"Provision boats," this time answered the Highlander. "Don't make a noise. The English will hear us."

That hint was enough, for an English sloop of war lay within sound of their voices.

With the swift tide the boats shot around a headland, and here was a cove in the huge precipice, clothed with sere herbage and bushes and a few trees; steep, with the hint of a once-used path across it, but a little less perpendicular than the rest of the rock. No sentinel was stationed at this place.

The world was just beginning to come out of positive shadow into the indistinctness of dawn. Current and tide were so strong that the boats could not be steered directly to shore, but on the alluvial strip at the base of this cove they beached themselves with such success as they could. Twenty-four men sprung out and ran to the ascent. Their muskets were slung upon their backs. A humid look was coming upon the earth, and blurs were over the fading stars. The climbers separated, each making his own way from point to point of the slippery cliff, and swarms followed them as boat after boat discharged its load. The cove by which he breached the stronghold of this continent, and which was from that day to bear his name, cast its shadow on the gaunt, upturned face of Wolfe. He waited while the troops in whom he put his trust, with knotted muscles and panting breasts, lifted themselves to the top. No orders were spoken. Wolfe had issued instructions the night before, and England expected every man to do his duty.

There was not enough light to show how Canada was taken. Jeannette Descheneaux stepped on the sand, and the single thought which took shape in her mind was that she must scale that ascent if the English scaled it.

The hope of escape to her own people did not animate her labor. She had no hope of any sort. She felt only present necessity, which was to climb where the Highland officer climbed. He was in front of her, and took no notice of her until they reached a slippery wall where there were no bushes. There he turned and caught her by the wrist, drawing her up after him. Their faces came near together in the swimming vapors of dawn. He had the bright look of determination. His eyes shone. He was about to burst into the man's arena of glory. The woman, whom he drew up because she was a woman, and because he regretted having taken her prisoner, had the pallid look of a victim. Her tragic black eyes and brows, and the hairs clinging in untidy threads about her haggard cheeks instead of curling up with the damp as the Highlandman's fleece inclined to do, worked an instant's compassion in him. But his business was not the squiring of angular Frenchwomen. Shots were heard at the top of the rock, a trampling rush, and then exulting shouts. The English had taken Vergor's camp.

The hand was gone from Jeannette's wrist, — the hand which gave her such rapture and such pain by its firm fraternal grip. Colonel Fraser leaped to the plain, and was in the midst of the skirmish. Cannon spoke, like thunder rolling across one's head. A battery guarded by the sentinels they had passed was aroused, and must be silenced. The whole face of the cliff suddenly bloomed with scarlet uniforms. All the men remaining in the boats went up as fire sweeps when carried by the wind. Nothing could restrain them. They smelled gunpowder and heard the noise of victory, and would have stormed heaven at that instant. They surrounded Jeannette without seeing her, every man looking up to the heights of glory, and passed her in fierce and panting emulation.

Jeannette leaned against the rough side of Wolfe's Cove. On the inner surface of her eyelids she could see again the image of the Highlandman stooping to help her, his muscular legs and neck showing like a young god's in the early light. There she lost him, for he forgot her. The passion of women whom nature has made unfeminine, and who are too honest to stoop to arts, is one of the tragedies of the world.

Daylight broke reluctantly, with clouds mustering from the inverted deep of the sky. A few drops of rain sprinkled the British uniforms as battalions were formed. The battery which gave the first intimation of danger to the French general, on the other side of Quebec, had been taken and silenced. Wolfe and his officers hurried up the high plateau and chose their ground. Then the troops advanced, marching by files, Highland bagpipes screaming and droning, the earth reverberating with a measured tread. As they moved toward Quebec they wheeled to form their line of battle, in ranks three deep, and stretched across the plain. The city was scarcely a mile away, but a ridge of ground still hid it from sight.

From her hiding-place in one of the empty houses behind Vergor's tents, Jeannette Descheneaux watched the scarlet backs and the tartans of the Highlanders grow smaller. She could also see the prisoners that were taken standing under guard. As for herself, she felt that she had no longer a visible presence, so easy had it been for her to move among swarms of men and escape in darkness. She never had favored her body with soft usage, but it trembled now in every part from muscular strain. She was probably cold and hungry, but her poignant sensation was that she had no friends. It did not matter to Jeannette that history was being made before her, and one of the great battles of the world was about to be fought. It only mattered that she should discern the Fraser plaid as far as eye could follow it. There is no more piteous thing than for one human being to be overpowered by the god in another.

She sat on the ground in the unfloored hut, watching through broken chinking. There was a back door as well as a front door, hung on wooden hinges, and she had pinned the front door as she came in. The opening of the back door made Jeannette turn her head, though with little interest in the comer. It was a boy, with a streak of blood down his face and neck, and his clothes stained by the weather. He had no hat on, and one of his shoes was missing. He put himself at Jeannette's side without any hesitation, and joined her watch through the broken chinking. A tear and a drop of scarlet raced down his cheek, uniting as they dripped from his chin.

"Have you been wounded?" inquired Jeannette.

"It is n't the wound," he answered, "but

that Captain Vergor has let them take the heights. I heard something myself, and tried to wake him. The pig turned over and went to sleep again."

"Let me tie it up," said Jeannette.

"He is shot in the heel and taken prisoner. I wish he had been shot in the heart. He hopped out of bed and ran away when the English fired on his tent. I have been trying to get past their lines to run to General Montcalm; but they are everywhere," declared the boy, his chin shaking and his breast swelling with grief.

Jeannette turned her back on him, and found some linen about her person which she could tear. She made a bandage for his head. It comforted her to take hold of the little fellow and part his clotted hair.

"The skin of my head is torn," he admitted, while suffering the attempted surgery. "If I had been taller, the bullet might have killed me; and I would rather be killed than see the English on this rock, marching to take Quebec. What will my father say? I am ashamed to look him in the face and own I slept in the camp of Vergor last night. The Le Moynes and Repentignys never let enemies get past them before. And I knew that man was not keeping watch; he did not set any sentry."

"Is it painful?" she inquired, wiping the bloody cut, which still welled forth along its channel.

The boy lifted his brimming eyes, and answered her from his deeper hurt: —

"I don't know what to do. I think my father would make for General Montcalm's camp if he were alone and could not attack the enemy's rear; for something ought to be done as quickly as possible."

Jeannette bandaged his head, the rain spattering through the broken log house upon them both.

"Who brought you here?" inquired Jacques. "There was nobody in these houses last night, for I searched them myself."

"I hid here before daybreak," she answered briefly.

"But if you knew the English were coming, why did you not give the alarm?"

"I was their prisoner."

"And where will you go now?"

She looked towards the Plains of Abraham and said nothing. The open chink showed Wolfe's six battalions of scarlet lines moving forward or pausing, and the ridge above them thronging with white uniforms.

"If you will trust yourself to me, mamoiselle," proposed Jacques, who considered that it was not the part of a soldier or a gentleman to leave any woman alone in this hut to take the chances of battle, and particularly a woman who had bound up his head, "I will do my best to help you inside the French lines."

The singular woman did not reply to him, but continued looking through the chink. Skirmishers were out. Puffs of smoke from cornfields and knolls showed where

Canadians and Indians hid, creeping to the flank of the enemy.

Jacques stooped down himself, and struck his hands together at these sights.

"Monsieur de Montcalm is awake, mademoiselle! And see our sharpshooters picking them off! We can easily run inside the French lines now. These English will soon be tumbled back the way they came up."

In another hour the group of houses was a roaring furnace. A detachment of English light infantry, wheeled to drive out the bushfighters, had lost and retaken it many times, and neither party gave up the ready fortress until it was set on fire. Crumbling red logs hissed in the thin rain, and smoke spread from them across the sodden ground where Wolfe moved. The sick man had become an invincible spirit. He flew along the ranks, waving his sword, the sleeve falling away from his thin arm. The great soldier had thrown himself on this venture without a chance of retreat, but every risk had been thought of and met. He had a battalion guarding the landing. He had a force far in the rear to watch the motions of the French at Cap Rouge. By the arrangement of his front he had taken precautions against being outflanked. And he knew his army was with him to a man. But Montcalm rode up to meet him hampered by insubordinate confusion.

Jeannette Descheneaux, carried along, with the boy, by Canadians and Indians from the English rear to the Côte Ste. Genevieve, lay dazed in the withered grass during the greater part of the action which decided her people's hold on the New World. The ground resounded like a drum with measured treading. The blaze and crash of musketry and cannon blinded and deafened her; but when she lifted her head from the shock of the first charge, the most instantaneous and shameful panic that ever seized a French army had already begun. The skirmishers in the bushes could not understand it. Smoke parted, and she saw the white-and-gold French general trying to drive his men back. But they evaded the horses of officers.

Jacques rose, with the Canadians and Indians, to his knees. He had a musket. Jeannette rose, also, as the Highlanders came sweeping on in pursuit. She had scarcely been a woman to the bushfighters. They were too eager in their aim to glance aside at a rawboned camp follower in a wet shawl. Neither did the Highlanders distinguish from other Canadian heads the one with a woman's braids and a faint shadowing of hair at the corners of the mouth. They came on without suspecting an ambush, and she heard their strange cries — "Cath-Shairm!" and "Caisteal Duna!" — when the shock of a volley stopped the streaming tartans. She saw the play of surprise and fury in those mountaineer faces. They threw down their muskets, and turned on the ambushed Canadians, short sword in hand.

Never did knight receive the blow of the

accolade as that crouching woman took a Highland knife in her breast. For one breath she grasped the back of it with both hands, and her rapt eyes met the horrified eyes of Colonel Fraser. He withdrew the weapon, standing defenseless, and a ball struck him, cutting the blood across his arm, and again he was lost in the fury of battle, while Jeannette felt herself dragged down the slope.

She resisted. She heard a boy's voice pleading with her, but she got up and tried to go back to the spot from which she had been dragged. The Canadians and Indians were holding their ground. She heard their muskets, but they were far behind her, and the great rout caught her and whirled her. Officers on their horses were borne struggling along in it. She fell down and was trampled on, but something helped her up.

The flood of men poured along the front of the ramparts and down to the bridge of boats on the St. Charles, or into the city walls through the St. Louis and St. John gates.

To Jeannette the world was far away. Yet she found it once more close at hand, as she stood with her back against the lofty inner wall. The mad crowd had passed, and gone shouting down the narrow streets. But the St. Louis gate was still choked with fugitives when Montcalm appeared, reeling on his horse, supported by a soldier on each side. His white uniform was stained on the breast, and blood dripped from the saddle. Jeannette heard the piercing cry of a little girl: "Oh heavens! Oh heavens! The marquis is killed!" And she heard the fainting general gasp, "It is nothing, it is nothing. Don't be troubled for me, my children."

She knew how he felt as he was led by. The indistinctness of the opposite wall, which widened from the gate, was astonishing. And she was troubled by the same little boy whose head she had tied up in the log house. Jeannette looked obliquely down at him as she braced herself with chill fingers, and discerned that he was claimed by a weeping little girl to whom he yet paid no attention.

"Let me help you, mademoiselle," he urged, troubling her.

"Go away," said Jeannette.

"But, mademoiselle, you have been badly hurt."

"Go away," said Jeannette, and her limbs began to settle. She thought of smiling at the children, but her features were already cast. The English child held her on one side, and the French child on the other, as she collapsed in a sitting posture. Tender nuns, going from friend to foe, would find this stoical face against the wall. It was no strange sight then. Canada was taken.

Men with bloody faces were already running with barricades for the gates. Wailing for Montcalm could be heard.

The boy put his arm around the girl and turned her eyes away. They ran together up towards the citadel: England and France with their hands locked; young Canada weeping, but having a future.

THE WINDIGO.

The cry of those rapids in Ste. Marie's River called the Sault could be heard at all hours through the settlement on the rising shore and into the forest beyond. Three quarters of a mile of frothing billows, like some colossal instrument, never ceased playing music down an inclined channel until the trance of winter locked it up. At August dusk, when all that shaggy world was sinking to darkness, the gushing monotone became very distinct.

Louizon Cadotte and his father's young seignior, Jacques de Repentigny, stepped from a birch canoe on the bank near the fort, two Chippewa Indians following with their game. Hunting furnished no small addition to the food supply of the settlement, for the English conquest had brought about scarcity at this as well as other West ern posts. Peace was declared in Europe; but soldiers on the frontier, waiting orders to march out at any time, were not abundantly supplied with stores, and they let season after season go by, reluctant to put in harvests which might be reaped by their successors.

Jacques was barely nineteen, and Louizon was considerably older. But the Repentignys had gone back to France after the fall of Quebec; and five years of European life had matured the young seignior as decades of border experience would never mature his half-breed tenant. Yet Louizon was a fine dark-skinned fellow, well made for one of short stature. He trod close by his tall superior with visible fondness; enjoying this spectacle of a man the like of whom he had not seen on the frontier.

Jacques looked back, as he walked, at the long zigzag shadows on the river. Forest fire in the distance showed a leaning column, black at base, pearl-colored in the primrose air, like smoke from some gigantic altar. He had seen islands in the lake under which the sky seemed to slip, throwing them above the horizon in mirage, and trees standing like detached bushes on a world rim of water. The Ste. Marie River was a beautiful light green in color, and sunset and twilight played upon it all the miracles of change.

"I wish my father had never left this country," said young Repentigny, feeling that spell cast by the wilderness. "Here is his place. He should have withdrawn to the Sault, and accommodated himself to the English, instead of returning to France. The service in other parts of the world does not suit him. Plenty of good men have held to Canada and their honor also."

"Yes, yes," assented Louizon. "The English cannot be got rid of. For my part, I shall be glad when this post changes hands. I am sick of our officers."

He scowled with open resentment. The seigniory house faced the parade ground, and they could see against its large low mass, lounging on the gallery, one each side of a window, the white uniforms of two French soldiers. The window sashes, screened by small curtains across the middle, were swung into the room; and Louizon's wife leaned on her elbows across the sill, the rosy atmosphere of his own fire projecting to view every ring of her bewitching hair, and even her long eyelashes as she turned her gaze from side to side.

It was so dark, and the object of their regard was so bright, that these buzzing bees of Frenchmen did not see her husband until he ran up the steps facing them. Both of them greeted him heartily. He felt it a peculiar indignity that his wife's danglers forever passed their good-will on to him; and he left them in the common hall, with his father and the young seignior, and the two or three Indians who congregated there every evening to ask for presents or to smoke.

Louizon's wife met him in the middle of the broad low apartment where he had been so proud to introduce her as a bride, and turned her cheek to be kissed. She was not fond of having her lips touched. Her hazel-colored hair was perfumed. She was so supple and exquisite, so dimpled and aggravating, that the Chippewa in him longed to take her by the scalp-lock of her light head; but the Frenchman bestowed the salute. Louizon had married the prettiest woman in the settlement. Life overflowed in her, so that her presence spread animation. Both men and women paid homage to her. Her very mother-in-law was her slave. And this was the stranger spectacle because Madame Cadotte the senior, though born a Chippewa, did not easily make herself subservient to anybody.

The time had been when Louizon was proud of any notice this siren conferred on him. But so exacting and tyrannical is the nature of man that when he got her he wanted to keep her entirely to himself. From his Chippewa mother, who, though treated with deference, had never dared to disobey his father, he inherited a fond and jealous nature; and his beautiful wife chafed it. Young Repentigny saw that she was like a Parisian. But Louizon felt that she was a spirit too fine and tantalizing for him to grasp, and she had him in her power.

He hung his powderhorn behind the door, and stepped upon a stool to put his gun on its rack above the fireplace. The fire showed his round figure, short but well muscled, and the boyish petulance of his shaven lip. The sun shone hot upon the Sault of an August noon, but morning and night were cool, and a blaze was usually kept in the chimney.

"You found plenty of game?" said his wife; and it was one of this woman's wickedest charms that she could be so interested in her companion of the moment.

"Yes," he answered, scowling more, and thinking of the brace on the gallery whom he had not shot, but wished to.

She laughed at him.

"Archange Cadotte," said Louizon, turning around on the stool before he descended; and she spread out her skirts, taking two dancing steps to indicate that she heard him. "How long am I to be mortified by your conduct to Monsieur de Repentigny?"

"Oh— Monsieur de Repentigny. It is now that boy from France, at whom I have never looked."

"The man I would have you look at, madame, you scarcely notice."

"Why should I notice him? He pays little attention to me."

"Ah, he is not one of your danglers, madame. He would not look at another man's wife. He has had trouble himself."

"So will you have if you scorch the backs of your legs," observed Archange.

Louizon stood obstinately on the stool and ignored the heat. He was in the act of stepping down, but he checked it as she spoke.

"Monsieur de Repentigny came back to this country to marry a young English lady of Quebec. He thinks of her, not of you."

"I am sure he is welcome," murmured Archange. "But it seems the young English lady prefers to stay in Quebec."

"She never looked at any other man, madame. She is dead."

"No wonder. I should be dead, too, if I had looked at one stupid man all my life."

Louizon's eyes sparkled. "Madame, I will have you know that the seignior of Sault Ste. Marie is entitled to your homage."

"Monsieur, I will have you know that I do not pay homage to any man."

"You, Archange Cadotte? You are in love with a new man every day."

"Not in the least, monsieur. I only desire to have a new man in love with me every day."

Her mischievous mouth was a scarlet button in her face, and Louizon leaped to the floor, and kicked the stool across the room.

"The devil himself is no match at all for you!"

"But I married him before I knew that," returned Archange; and Louizon grinned in his wrath.

"I don't like such women."

"Oh yes, you do. Men always like women whom·they cannot chain."

"I have never tried to chain you." Her husband approached, shaking his finger at her. "There is not another woman in the settlement who has her way as you have. And see how you treat me!"

"How do I treat you?" inquired Archange, sitting down and resigning herself to statistics.

"Ste. Marie! St. Joseph!" shouted the Frenchman. "How does she treat me! And every man in the seigniory dangling at her apron string!"

"You are mistaken. There is the young seignior; and there is the new English commandant, who must be now within the seigniory, for they expect him at the post to-morrow morning. It is all the same: if I look at a man you are furious, and if I refuse to look at him you are more furious still."

Louizon felt that inward breaking up which proved to him that he could not stand before the tongue of this woman. Groping for expression, he declared, —

"If thou wert sickly or blind, I would be just as good to thee as when thou wert a bride. I am not the kind that changes if a woman loses her fine looks."

"No doubt you would like to see me with the smallpox," suggested Archange. "But it is never best to try a man too far."

"You try me too far, — let me tell you that. But you shall try me no further."

The Indian appeared distinctly on his softer French features, as one picture may be stamped over another.

"Smoke a pipe, Louizon," urged the thorn in his flesh. "You are always so much more agreeable when your mouth is stopped."

But he left the room without looking at her again. Archange remarked to herself that he would be better natured when his mother had given him his supper; and she yawned, smiling at the maladroit creatures whom she made her sport. Her husband was the best young man in the settlement. She was entirely satisfied with him, and grateful to him for taking the orphan niece of a poor post commandant, without prospects since the conquest, and giving her sumptuous quarters and comparative wealth; but she could not forbear amusing herself with his masculine weaknesses.

Archange was by no means a slave in the frontier household. She did not spin, or draw water, or tend the oven. Her mother-in-law, Madame Cadotte, had a hold on perennially destitute Chippewa women who could be made to work for longer or shorter periods in a Frenchman's kitchen or loom-house instead of with savage implements. Archange's bed had ruffled curtains, and her pretty dresses, carefully folded, filled a large chest.

She returned to the high window sill, and watched the purple distances growing black. She could smell the tobacco the men were smoking in the open hall, and hear their voices. Archange knew what her mother-in-law was giving the young seignior and Louizon for their supper. She could fancy the officers laying down their pipes to draw to the board, also, for the Cadottes kept open house all the year round.

The thump of the Indian drum was added to the deep melody of the rapids. There were always a few lodges of Chippewas about the Sault. When the trapping season and the maple-sugar making were over and his profits drunk up, time was the largest possession of an Indian. He spent it around the door of his French brother, ready to fish or to drink whenever invited. If no one cared to go on the river, he turned to his hereditary amusements. Every night that the rapids were void of torches showing where the canoes of white fishers darted, the thump of the Indian drum and the yell of Indian dancers could be heard.

Archange's mind was running on the new English garrison who were said to be so near taking possession of the picketed fort, when she saw something red on the parade ground. The figure stood erect and motionless, gathering all the remaining light on its indistinct coloring, and Archange's heart gave a leap at the hint of a military man in a red uniform. She was all alive, like a whitefisher casting the net or a hunter sighting game. It was Archange's nature, without even taking thought, to turn her head on her round neck so that the illuminated curls would show against a background of wall, and wreathe her half-bare arms across the sill. To be looked at, to lure and tantalize, was more than pastime. It was a woman's chief privilege. Archange held the secret conviction that the priest himself could be made to give her lighter penances by an angelic expression she could assume. It is convenient to have large brown eyes and the trick of casting them sidewise in sweet distress.

But the Chippewa widow came in earlier than usual that evening, being anxious to go back to the lodges to watch the dancing. Archange pushed the sashes shut, ready for other diversion, and Michel Pensonneau never failed to furnish her that. The little boy was at the widow's heels. Michel was an orphan.

"If Archange had children," Madame Cadotte had said to Louizon, "she would not seek other amusement. Take the little Pensonneau lad that his grandmother can hardly feed. He will give Archange something to do."

So Louizon brought home the little Pensonneau lad. Archange looked at him, and considered that here was another person to wait on her. As to keeping him clean and making clothes for him, they might as well have expected her to train the sledge dogs. She made him serve her, but for mothering he had to go to Madame Cadotte. Yet Archange far outweighed Madame Cadotte with him. The labors put upon him by the autocrat of the house were sweeter than mococks full of maple sugar from the hand of the Chippewa housekeeper. At first Archange would not let him come into her room. She dictated to him through door or window. But when he grew fat with good food and was decently clad under Madame Cadotte's hand, the great promotion of entering that sacred apartment was allowed him. Michel came in whenever he could. It was his nightly habit to follow the Chippewa widow there after supper, and watch her brush Archange's hair.

Michel stood at the end of the hearth with a roll of pagessanung or plum-leather in his fist. His cheeks had a hard garnered redness like polished apples. The Chippewa widow set her husband carefully against the wall. The husband was a bundle about two feet long, containing her best clothes tied up in her dead warrior's sashes and rolled in a piece of cloth. His armbands and his necklace of bear's-claws appeared at the top as a grotesque head. This bundle the widow was obliged to carry with her everywhere. To be seen without it was a disgrace, until that time when her husband's nearest relations should take it away from her and give her new clothes, thus signifying that she had mourned long enough to satisfy them. As the husband's relations were unable to cover themselves, the prospect of her release seemed distant. For her food she was glad to depend on her labor in the Cadotte household. There was no hunter to supply her lodge now.

The widow let down Archange's hair and began to brush it. The long mass was too much for its owner to handle. It spread around her like a garment, as she sat on her chair, and its ends touched the floor. Michel thought there was nothing more wonderful in the world than this glory of hair, its rings and ripples shining in the firelight. The widow's jaws worked in unobtrusive rumination on a piece of pleasantly bitter fungus, the Indian substitute for quinine, which the Chippewas called waubudone. As she consoled herself much with this medicine, and her many-syllabled name was hard to pronounce, Archange called her Waubudone, an offense against her dignity which the widow might not have endured from anybody else, though she bore it without a word from this soft-haired magnate.

As she carefully carded the mass of hair lock by lock, thinking it an unnecessary nightly labor, the restless head under her hands was turned towards the portable husband. Archange had not much imagination, but to her the thing was uncanny. She repeated what she said every night:—

"Do stand him in the hall and let him smell the smoke, Waubudone."

"No," refused the widow.

"But I don't want him in my bedroom. You are not obliged to keep that thing in your sight all the time."

"Yes," said the widow.

A dialect of mingled French and Chippewa was what they spoke, and Michel knew enough of both tongues to follow the talk.

"Are they never going to take him from you? If they don't take him from you soon, I shall go to the lodges and speak to his people about it myself."

The Chippewa widow usually passed over this threat in silence; but, threading a lock with the comb, she now said, —

"Best not go to the lodges awhile."

"Why?" inquired Archange. "Have the English already arrived? Is the tribe dissatisfied?"

"Don't know that."

"Then why should I not go to the lodges?"

"Windigo at the Sault now."

Archange wheeled to look at her face. The widow was unmoved. She was little older than Archange, but her features showed a stoical harshness in the firelight.

Michel, who often went to the lodges, widened his mouth and forgot to fill it with plum-leather. There was no sweet which Michel loved as he did this confection of wild plums and maple sugar boiled down and spread on sheets of birch bark. Madame Cadotte made the best pagessanung at the Sault.

"Look at the boy," laughed Archange. "He will not want to go to the lodges any more after dark."

The widow remarked, noting Michel's fat legs and arms, —

"Windigo like to eat him."

"I would kill a windigo," declared Michel, in full revolt.

"Not so easy to kill a windigo. Bad spirits help windigos. If man kill windigo and not tear him to pieces, he come to life again."

Archange herself shuddered at such a tenacious creature. She was less superstitious than the Chippewa woman, but the Northwest had its human terrors as dark as the shadow of witchcraft.

Though a Chippewa was bound to dip his hand in the war kettle and taste the flesh of enemies after victory, there was nothing he considered more horrible than a confirmed cannibal. He believed that a person who had eaten human flesh to satisfy hunger was never afterwards contented with any other kind, and, being deranged and possessed by the spirit of a beast, he had to be killed for the safety of the community. The cannibal usually became what he was by stress of starvation: in the winter when hunting failed and he was far from help, or on a journey when provisions gave out, and his only choice was to eat a companion or die. But this did not excuse him. As soon as he was detected the name of "windigo" was given him, and if he did not betake himself again to solitude he was shot or knocked on the head at the first convenient opportunity. Archange remembered one such wretched creature who had haunted the settlement awhile, and then disappeared. His canoe was known, and when it hovered even distantly on the river every child ran to its mother. The priest was less successful with this kind of outcast than with any other barbarian on the frontier.

"Have you seen him, Waubudone?" inquired Archange. "I wonder if it is the same man who used to frighten us?"

"This windigo a woman. Porcupine in her. She lie down and roll up and hide her head when you drive her off."

"Did you drive her off?"

"No. She only come past my lodge in the night."

"Did you see her?"

"No, I smell her."

Archange had heard of the atmosphere which windigos far gone in cannibalism carried around them. She desired to know nothing more about the poor creature, or the class to which the poor creature belonged, if such isolated beings may be classed. The Chippewa widow talked without being questioned, however, preparing to reduce Archange's mass of hair to the compass of a nightcap.

"My grandmother told me there was a man dreamed he had to eat seven persons. He sat by the fire and shivered. If his squaw wanted meat, he quarreled with her. 'Squaw, take care. Thou wilt drive me so far that I shall turn windigo.'"

People who did not give Archange the keen interest of fascinating them were a great weariness to her. Humble or wretched human life filled her with disgust. She could dance all night at the weekly dances, laughing in her sleeve at girls from whom she took the best partners. But she never helped nurse a sick child, and it made her sleepy to hear of windigos and misery. Michel wanted to squat by the chimney and listen until Louizon came in; but she drove him out early. Louizon was kind to the orphan, who had been in some respects a failure, and occasionally let him sleep on blankets or skins by the hearth instead of groping to the dark attic. And if Michel ever wanted to escape the attic, it was tonight, when a windigo was abroad. But Louizon did not come.

It must have been midnight when Archange sat up in bed, startled out of sleep by her mother-in-law, who held a candle between the curtains. Madame Cadotte's features were of a mild Chippewa type, yet the restless aboriginal eye made Archange uncomfortable with its anxiety.

"Louizon is still away," said his mother.

"Perhaps he went whitefishing after he had his supper." The young wife yawned and rubbed her eyes, beginning to notice that her husband might be doing something unusual.

"He did not come to his supper."

"Yes, mama. He came in with Monsieur de Repentigny."

"I did not see him. The seignior ate alone."

Archange stared, fully awake. "Where does the seignior say he is?"

"The seignior does not know. They parted at the door."

"Oh, he has gone to the lodges to watch the dancing."

"I have been there. No one has seen him since he set out to hunt this morning."

"Where are Louizon's canoemen?"

"Jean Boucher and his son are at the dancing. They say he came into this house."

Archange could not adjust her mind to anxiety without the suspicion that her mother-in-law might be acting as the instrument of Louizon's resentment. The huge feather bed was a tangible comfort interposed betwixt herself and calamity.

"He was sulky to-night," she declared. "He has gone up to sleep in Michel's attic to frighten me."

"I have been there. I have searched the house."

"But are you sure it was Michel in the bed?"

"There was no one. Michel is here."

Archange snatched the curtain aside, and leaned out to see the orphan sprawled on a bearskin in front of the collapsing logs. He had pushed the sashes inward from the gallery and hoisted himself over the high sill after the bed drapery was closed for the night, for the window yet stood open. Madame Cadotte sheltered the candle she carried, but the wind blew it out. There was a rich glow from the fireplace upon Michel's stuffed legs and arms, his cheeks, and the full parted lips through which his breath audibly flowed. The other end of the room, lacking the candle, was in shadow. The thump of the Indian drum could still be heard, and distinctly and more distinctly, as if they were approaching the house, the rapids.

Both women heard more. They had not noticed any voice at the window when they were speaking themselves, but some offensive thing scented the wind, and they heard, hoarsely spoken in Chippewa from the gallery, —

"How fat he is!"

Archange, with a gasp, threw herself

upon her mother-in-law for safety, and Madame Cadotte put both arms and the smoking candle around her. A feeble yet dexterous scramble on the sill resulted in something dropping into the room. It moved toward the hearth glow, a gaunt vertebrate body scarcely expanded by ribs, but covered by a red blanket, and a head with deathlike features overhung by strips of hair. This vision of famine leaned forward and indented Michel with one finger, croaking again, —

" How fat he is ! "

The boy roused himself, and, for one instant stupid and apologetic, was going to sit up and whine. He saw what bent over him, and, bristling with unimaginable revolutions of arms and legs, he yelled a yell which seemed to sweep the thing back through the window.

Next day no one thought of dancing or fishing or of the coming English. Frenchmen and Indians turned out together to search for Louizon Cadotte. Though he never in his life had set foot to any expedition without first notifying his household, and it was not the custom to hunt alone in the woods, his disappearance would not have roused the settlement in so short a time had there been no windigo hanging about the Sault. It was told that the windigo, who entered his house again in the night, must have made way with him.

Jacques Repentigny heard this with some amusement. Of windigos he had no experience, but he had hunted and camped much of the summer with Louizon.

"I do not think he would let himself be knocked on the head by a woman," said Jacques.

"White chief does n't know what helps a windigo," explained a Chippewa; and the canoeman Jean Boucher interpreted him. "Bad spirit makes a windigo strong as a bear. I saw this one. She stole my whitefish and ate them raw."

"Why did n't you give her cooked food when you saw her?" demanded Jacques.

"She would not eat that now. She likes offal better."

"Yes, she was going to eat me," declared Michel Pensonneau. "After she finished Monsieur Louizon, she got through the window to carry me off."

Michel enjoyed the windigo. Though he strummed on his lip and mourned aloud whenever Madame Cadotte was by, he felt so comfortably full of food and horror, and so important with his story, that life threatened him with nothing worse than satiety.

While parties went up the river and down the river, and talked about the chutes in the rapids where a victim could be sucked down to death in an instant, or about tracing the windigo's secret camp, Archange hid herself in the attic. She lay upon Michel's bed and wept, or walked the plank floor. It was no place for her. At noon the bark roof heated her almost to fever. The dormer windows gave her little air, and there was dust as well as something like an individual sediment of the poverty from which the boy had come. Yet she could endure the loft dungeon better than the face of the Chippewa mother who blamed her, or the bluff excitement of Monsieur Cadotte. She could hear his voice from time to time, as he ran in for spirits or provisions for parties of searchers. And Archange had aversion, like the instinct of a maid, to betraying fondness for her husband. She was furious with him, also, for causing her pain. When she thought of the windigo, of the rapids, of any peril which might be working his limitless absence, she set clenched hands in her loosened hair and trembled with hysterical anguish. But the enormity of his behavior if he were alive made her hiss at the rafters. "Good, monsieur! Next time I will have four officers. I will have the entire garrison sitting along the gallery! Yes, and they shall be English, too. And there is one thing you will never know, besides." She laughed through her weeping. "You will never know I made eyes at a windigo."

The preenings and posings of a creature whose perfections he once thought were the result of a happy chance had made Louizon roar. She remembered all their life together, and moaned, "I will say this: he was the best husband that any girl ever had. We scarcely had a disagreement. But to be the widow of a man who is eaten up — O Ste. Marie!"

In the clear August weather the wide river seemed to bring its opposite shores nearer. Islands within a stone's throw of the settlement, rocky drops in a boiling current, vividly showed their rich foliage of pines. On one of these islands Father Dablon and Father Marquette had built their first mission chapel; and though they afterwards removed it to the mainland, the old tracery of foundation stones could still be seen. The mountains of Lake Superior showed like a cloud. On the ridge above fort and houses the Chippewa lodges were pleasant in the sunlight, sending ribbons of smoke from their camp fires far above the serrated edge of the woods. Naked Indian children and their playmates of the settlement shouted to one another, as they ran along the river margin, threats of instant seizure by the windigo. The Chippewa widow, holding her husband in her arms, for she was not permitted to hang him on her back, stood and talked with her red-skinned intimates of the lodges. The Frenchwomen collected at the seigniory house. As for the men of the garrison, they were obliged to stay and receive the English then on the way from Detour. But they came out to see the boats off with the concern of brothers, and Archange's uncle, the post commandant, embraced Monsieur Cadotte.

The priest and Jacques Repentigny did not speak to each other about that wretched creature whose hoverings around the Sault were connected with Louizon Cadotte's disappearance. But the priest went with Louizon's father down the river, and Jacques led the party which took the opposite direction. Though so many years had passed since Father Dablon and Father Marquette built the first bark chapel, their successor found his work very little easier than theirs had been.

A canoe was missing from the little fleet usually tied alongshore, but it was not the one belonging to Louizon. The young seignior took that one, having Jean Boucher and Jean's son to paddle for him. No other man of Sault Ste. Marie could pole up the rapids or paddle down them as this expert Chippewa could. He had been baptized with a French name, and his son after him, but no Chippewa of pure blood and name looked habitually as he did into those whirlpools called the chutes, where the slip of a paddle meant death. Yet nobody feared the rapids. It was common for boys and girls to flit around near shore in birch canoes, balancing themselves and expertly dipping up whitefish.

Jean Boucher thrust out his boat from behind an island, and, turning it as a fish glides, moved over thin sheets of water spraying upon rocks. The fall of the Ste. Marie is gradual, but even at its upper end there is a little hill to climb. Jean set his pole into the stone floor of the river, and lifted the vessel length by length from crest to crest of foam. His paddles lay behind him, and his arms were bare to the elbows, showing their strong red sinews. He had let his hair grow like a Frenchman's, and it hung forward shading his hatless brows. A skin apron was girded in front of him to meet waves which frothed up over the canoe's high prow. Blacksmith of the waters, he beat a path between juts of rock; struggling to hold a point with the pole, calling a quick word to his helper, and laughing as he forged his way. Other voyagers who did not care to tax themselves with this labor made a portage with their canoes alongshore, and started above the glassy curve where the river bends down to its leap.

Gros Cap rose in the sky, revealing its

peak in bolder lines as the searchers pushed up the Ste. Marie, exploring mile after mile of pine and white birch and fantastic rock. The shaggy bank stooped to them, the illimitable glory of the wilderness witnessing a little procession of boats like chips floating by.

It was almost sunset when they came back, the tired paddlers keeping near that shore on which they intended to land. No trace of Louizon Cadotte could be found; and those who had not seen the windigo were ready to declare that there was no such thing about the Sault, when, just above the rapids, she appeared from the dense up-slope of forest.

Jacques Repentigny's canoe had kept the lead, but a dozen light-bodied Chippewas sprung on shore and rushed past him into the bushes.

The woman had disappeared in underbrush, but, surrounded by hunters in full chase, she came running out, and fell on her hands, making a hoarse noise in her throat.

As she looked up, all the marks in her aged aboriginal face were distinct to Jacques Repentigny. The sutures in her temples were parted. She rolled herself around in a ball, and hid her head in her dirty red blanket. Any wild beast was in harmony with the wilderness, but this sick human being was a blot upon it. Jacques felt the compassion of a god for her. Her pursuers were after her, and the thud of stones they threw made him heartsick, as if the thing were done to the woman he loved.

"Let her alone!" he commanded fiercely.

"Kill her!" shouted the hunters. "Hit the windigo on the head!"

All that world of northern air could not sweeten her, but Jacques picked her up without a thought of her offensiveness and ran to his canoe. The bones resisted him; the claws scratched at him through her blanket. Jean Boucher lifted a paddle to hit the creature as soon as she was down.

"If you strike her, I will kill you!"

warned Jacques, and he sprung into the boat.

The superstitious Chippewas threw themselves madly into their canoes to follow. It would go hard, but they would get the windigo and take the young seignior out of her spell. The Frenchmen, with man's instinct for the chase, were in full cry with them.

Jean Boucher laid down his paddle sulkily, and his son did the same. Jacques took a long pistol from his belt and pointed it at the old Indian.

"If you don't paddle for life, I will shoot you." And his eyes were eyes which Jean respected as he never had respected anything before. The young man was a beautiful fellow. If he wanted to save a windigo, why, the saints let him. The priest might say a good word about it when you came to think, also.

"Where shall I paddle to?" inquired Jean Boucher, drawing in his breath. The canoe leaped ahead, grazing hands stretched out to seize it.

"To the other side of the river."

"Down the rapids?"

"Yes."

"Go down rough or go down smooth?"

"Rough — rough — where they cannot catch you."

The old canoeman snorted. He would like to see any of them catch him. They were straining after him, and half a dozen canoes shot down that glassy slide which leads to the rocks.

It takes three minutes for a skillful paddler to run that dangerous race of three quarters of a mile. Jean Boucher stood at the prow, and the waves boiled as high as his waist. Jacques dreaded only that the windigo might move and destroy the delicate poise of the boat; but she lay very still. The little craft quivered from rock to rock without grazing one, rearing itself over a great breaker or sinking under a crest of foam. Now a billow towered up, and Jean broke it with his paddle, shouting his joy. Showers fell on the woman coiled in the bottom of the boat. They were going down very rough indeed. Yells from the other canoes grew less distinct. Jacques turned his head, keeping a true balance, and saw that their pursuers were skirting toward the shore. They must make a long detour to catch him after he reached the foot of the fall.

The roar of awful waters met him as he looked ahead. Jean Boucher drove the paddle down and spoke to his son. The canoe leaned sidewise, sucked by the first chute, a caldron in the river bed where all Ste. Marie's current seemed to go down, and whirl, and rise, and froth, and roar.

"Ha!" shouted Jean Boucher. His face glistened with beads of water and the glory of mastering Nature.

Scarcely were they past the first pit when the canoe plunged on the verge of another. This sight was a moment of madness. The great chute, lined with moving water walls and floored with whirling foam, bellowed as if it were submerging the world.

Columns of green water sheeted in white rose above it and fell forward on the current. As the canoemen held on with their paddles and shot by through spume and rain, every soul in the boat exulted except the woman who lay flat on its keel. The rapids gave a voyager the illusion that they were running uphill to meet him, that they were breasting and opposing him instead of carrying him forward. There was scarcely a breath between riding the edge of the bottomless pit and shooting out on clear water. The rapids were past, and they paddled for the other shore, a mile away.

On the west side the green water seemed turning to fire, but as the sunset went out, shadows sunk on the broad surface. The fresh evening breath of a primitive world blew across it. Down river the channel turned, and Jacques could see nothing of the English or of the other party. His pursuers had decided to land at the settlement.

It was twilight when Jean Boucher brought the canoe to pine woods which met them at the edge of the water. The young Repentigny had been wondering what he should do with his windigo. There was no settlement on this shore, and had there been one it would offer no hospitality to such as she was. His canoemen would hardly camp with her, and he had no provisions. To keep her from being stoned or torn to pieces he had made an inconsiderate flight. But his perplexity dissolved in a moment before the sight of Louizon Cadotte coming out of the woods towards them, having no hunting equipments and looking foolish.

"Where have you been?" called Jacques.

"Down this shore," responded Louizon.

"Did you take a canoe and come out here last night?"

"Yes, monsieur. I wished to be by myself. The canoe is below. I was coming home."

"It is time you were coming home, when all the men in the settlement are searching for you, and all the women trying to console your mother and your wife."

"My wife — she is not then talking with any one on the gallery?" Louizon's voice betrayed gratified revenge.

"I do not know. But there is a woman in this canoe who might talk on the gallery and complain to the priest against a man who has got her stoned on his account."

Louizon did not understand this, even when he looked at the heap of dirty blanket in the canoe.

"Who is it?" he inquired.

"The Chippewas call her a windigo. They were all chasing her for eating you up. But now we can take her back to the priest, and they will let her alone when they see you. Where is your canoe?"

"Down here among the bushes," answered Louizon. He went to get it, ashamed to look the young seignior in the face. He was light-headed from hunger and exposure, and what followed seemed to him afterwards a piteous dream.

"Come back!" called the young seignior, and Louizon turned back. The two men's eyes met in a solemn look.

"Jean Boucher says this woman is dead."

Jean Boucher stood on the bank, holding the canoe with one hand, and turning her unresisting face with the other. Jacques and Louizon took off their hats.

They heard the cry of the whip-poor-will. The river had lost all its green and was purple, and purple shadows lay on the distant mountains and opposite ridge. Darkness was mercifully covering this poor demented Indian woman, overcome by the burdens of her life, aged without being venerable, perhaps made hideous by want and sorrow.

When they had looked at her in silence, respecting her because she could no longer be hurt by anything in the world, Louizon whispered aside to his seignior, —

"What shall we do with her?"

"Bury her," the old canoeman answered for him.

One of the party yet thought of taking her back to the priest. But she did not belong to priests and rites. Jean Boucher said they could dig in the forest mould with a paddle, and he and his son would make her a grave. The two Chippewas left the burden to the young men.

Jacques Repentigny and Louizon Cadotte took up the woman who, perhaps had never been what they considered woman; who had missed the good, and got for her portion the ignorance and degradation of the world; yet who must be something to the Almighty, for he had sent youth and love to pity and take care of her in her death. They carried her into the woods between them.

THE KIDNAPED BRIDE.

(For this story, little changed from the form in which it was handed down to him, I am indebted to Dr. J. F. Snyder of Virginia, Illinois, a descendant of the Saucier family. Even the title remains unchanged, since he insisted on keeping the one always used by his uncle, Mathieu Saucier. "Mon Oncle Mathieu," he says, "I knew well, and often sat with breathless interest listening to his narration of incidents in the early settlement of the Bottom lands. He was a very quiet, dignified, and unobtrusive gentleman, and in point of common sense and intelligence much above the average of the race to which he belonged; but, like all the rest of the French stock, woefully wanting in energy and never in a hurry. He was a splendid fiddler, and consequently a favorite with all, especially the young folks, who easily pressed him into service on all occasions to play for their numerous dances. He died at Prairie du Pont, in 1863, at the age of eighty-one years. His mother, Manette Le Compt, then a young girl, was one of the bridesmaids of the kidnaped bride.")

Yes, the marshes were then in a chain along the foot of the bluffs: Grand Marais, Marais de Bois Coupé, Marais de l' Ourse, Marais Perdu; with a rigolé here and there, straight as a canal, to carry the water into the Mississippi. You do not see Cahokia beautiful as it was when Monsieur St. Ange de Bellerive was acting as governor of the Illinois Territory, and waiting at Fort Chartres for the British to take possession after the conquest. Some people had indeed gone off to Ste. Genevieve, and to Pain Court, that you now call Sah Loui', where Pontiac was afterwards buried under sweetbrier, and is to-day trampled under pavements. An Indian killed Pontiac between

Cahokia and Prairie du Pont. When he rose from his body and saw it was not a British knife, but a red man's tomahawk, he was not a chief who would lie still and bear it in silence. Yes, I have heard that he has been seen walking through the grapevine tangle, all bleached as if the bad redness was burned out of him. But the priest will tell you better, my son. Do not believe such tales.

Besides, no two stories are alike. Pontiac was killed in his French officer's uniform, which Monsieur de Montcalm gave him, and half the people who saw him walking declared he wore that, while the rest swore he was in buckskins and a blanket. You see how it is. A veritable ghost would always appear the same, and not keep changing its clothes like a vain girl. Paul Le Page had a fit one night from seeing the dead chief with feathers in his hair, standing like stone in the white French uniform. But do not credit such things.

It was half a dozen years before Pontiac's

death that Celeste Barbeau was kidnaped on her wedding day. She lived at Prairie du Pont; and though Prairie du Pont is but a mile and a half south of Cahokia, the road was not as safe then as it now is. My mother was one of the bridesmaids; she has told it over to me a score of times. The wedding was to be in the church; the same church that now stands on the east side of the square. And on the south side of the square was the old auberge. Claudis Beauvois said you could get as good wines at that tavern as you could in New Orleans. But the court-house was not built until 1795. The people did not need a court-house. They had no quarrels among themselves which the priest could not settle, and after the British conquest their only enemies were those Puants, the Pottawattamie Indians, who took the English side, and paid no regard when peace was declared, but still tormented the French because there was no military power to check them. You see the common fields across the rigolé. The

Puants stole stock from the common fields, they trampled down crops, and kidnaped children and even women, to be ransomed for so many horses each. The French tried to be friendly, and with presents and good words to induce the Puants to leave. But those Puants — Oh, they were British Indians: nothing but whipping would take the impudence out of them.

Celeste Barbeau's father and mother lived at Prairie du Pont, and Alexis Barbeau was the richest man in this part of the American Bottom. When Alexis Barbeau was down on his knees at mass, people used to say he counted his money instead of his beads; it was at least as dear to him as religion. And when he came au Caho',[1] he hadn't a word for a poor man. At Prairie du Pont he had built himself a fine brick house; the bricks were brought from Philadelphia by way of New Orleans. You have yourself seen it many a time, and the crack down the side made by the great earthquake of

[1] To Cahokia.

1811. There he lived like an estated gentleman, for Prairie du Pont was then nothing but a cluster of tenants around his feet. It was after his death that the village grew. Celeste did not stay at Prairie du Pont; she was always au Caho', with her grandmother and grandfather, the old Barbeaus.

Along the south bank of this rigolé which bounds the north end of Caho' were all the pleasantest houses then: rez-de-chaussée, of course, but large; with dormer windows in the roofs; and high of foundation, having flights of steps going up to the galleries. For though the Mississippi was a mile away in those days, and had not yet eaten in to our very sides, it often came visiting. I have seen this grassy-bottomed rigolé many a time swimming with fifteen feet of water, and sending ripples to the gallery steps. Between the marais and the Mississippi, the spring rains were a perpetual danger. There are men who want the marshes all filled up. They say it will add to us on one side what the great river is taking from us on the other; but myself — I would never throw in a shovelful: God made this world; it is good enough; and when the water rises we can take to boats.

The Le Compts lived in this very house, and the old Barbeaus lived next, on the corner, where this rigolé road crosses the street running north and south. Every house along the rigolé was set in spacious grounds, with shade trees and gardens, and the sloping lawns blazed with flowers. My mother said it was much prettier than Kaskaskia; not crowded with traffic; not overrun with foreigners. Everybody seemed to be making a fête, to be visiting or receiving visits. At sunset the fiddle and the banjo began their melody. The young girls would gather at Barbeau's or Le Compt's or Pensonneau's — at any one of a dozen places, and the young men would follow. It was no trouble to have a dance every evening, and on feast days and great days there were balls, of course. The violin ran in my family. Celeste Barbeau would call across the hedge to my mother, —

"Manette, will Monsieur Le Compt play for us again to-night?"

And Monsieur Le Compt or anybody who could handle a bow would play for her. Celeste was the life of the place: she sang like a lark, she was like thistledown in the dance, she talked well, and was so handsome that a stranger from New Orleans stopped in the street to gaze after her. At the auberge he said he was going au Pay,[1] but after he saw Celeste Barbeau he stayed in Caho'. I have heard my mother tell — who often saw it combed out — that Celeste's long black hair hung below her knees, though it was so curly that half its length was taken up by the natural crêping of the locks.

The old French women, especially about Pain Court and Caho', loved to go into their children's bedrooms and sit on the side of the bed, telling stories half the

[1] To Peoria.

night. It was part of the general good time. And thus they often found out what the girls were thinking about; for women of experience need only a hint. It is true old Madame Barbeau had never been even au Kaw;[1] but one may live and grow wise without crossing the rigolés north and south, or the bluffs and river east and west.

"Gra'mère, Manette is sleepy," Celeste would say, when my mother was with her.

"Well, I will go to my bed," the grandmother would promise. But still she sat and joined in the chatter. Sometimes the girls would doze, and wake in the middle of a long tale. But Madame Barbeau heard more than she told, for she said to her husband: —

"It may come to pass that the widow Chartrant's Gabriel will be making proposals to Alexis for little Celeste."

"Poor lad," said the grandfather, "he has nothing to back his proposals with. It will do him no good."

[1] To Kaskaskia.

And so it proved. Gabriel Chartrant was the leader of the young men as Celeste was of the girls. But he only inherited the cedar house his mother lived in. Those cedar houses were built in Caho' without an ounce of iron; each cedar shingle was held to its place with cedar pegs, and the boards of the floors fastened down in the same manner. They had their galleries, too, all tightly pegged to place. Gabriel was obliged to work, but he was so big he did not mind that. He was made very straight, with a high-lifted head and a full chest. He could throw any man in a wrestling match. And he was always first with a kindness, and would nurse the sick, and he was not afraid of contagious diseases or of anything. Gabriel could match Celeste as a dancer, but it was not likely Alexis Barbeau would find him a match in any other particular. And it grew more unlikely every day that the man from New Orleans spent in Caho'.

The stranger said his name was Claudis

Beauvois, and he was interested in great mercantile houses both in Philadelphia and New Orleans, and had come up the river to see the country. He was about fifty, a handsome, easy man, with plenty of fine clothes and money, and before he had been at the tavern a fortnight the hospitable people were inviting him everywhere, and he danced with the youngest of them all. There was about him what the city alone gives a man, and the mothers, when they saw his jewels, considered that there was only one drawback to marrying their daughters to Claudis Beauvois: his bride must travel far from Caho'.

But it was plain whose daughter he had fixed his mind upon, and Alexis Barbeau would not make any difficulty about parting with Celeste. She had lived away from him so much since her childhood that he would scarcely miss her; and it was better to have a daughter well settled in New Orleans than hampered by a poor match in her native village. And this was what

Gabriel Chartrant was told when he made haste to propose for Celeste about the same time.

"I have already accepted for my daughter much more gratifying offers than any you can make. The banns will be put up next Sunday, and in three weeks she will be Madame Beauvois."

When Celeste heard this she was beside herself. She used to tell my mother that Monsieur Beauvois walked as if his natural gait was on all fours, and he still took to it when he was not watched. His shoulders were bent forward, his hands were in his pockets, and he studied the ground. She could not endure him. But the customs were very strict in the matter of marriage. No French girl in those days could be so bold as to reject the husband her father picked, and own that she preferred some one else. Celeste was taken home to get ready for her wedding. She hung on my mother's neck when choosing her for a bridesmaid, and neither of the girls could comfort the other. Madame Barbeau was a fat woman who loved ease, and never interfered with Alexis. She would be disturbed enough by settling her daughter without meddling about bridegrooms. The grandfather and grandmother were sorry for Gabriel Chartrant, and tearful over Celeste; still, when you are forming an alliance for your child, it is very imprudent to disregard great wealth and by preference give her to poverty. Their son Alexis convinced them of this; and he had always prospered.

So the banns were put up in church for three weeks, and all Cahokia was invited to the grand wedding. Alexis Barbeau regretted there was not time to send to New Orleans for much that he wanted to fit his daughter out and provide for his guests.

"If he had sent there a month ago for some certainties about the bridegroom it might be better," said Paul Le Page. "I have a cousin in New Orleans who could have told us if he really is the great man he pretends to be." But the women said it was plain Paul Le Page was one of those who had wanted Celeste himself. The suspicious nature is a poison.

Gabriel Chartrant did not say anything for a week, but went along the streets haggard, though with his head up, and worked as if he meant to kill himself. The second week he spent his nights forming desperate plans. The young men followed him as they always did, and they held their meeting down the rigolé, clustered together on the bank. They could hear the frogs croak in the marais; it was dry, and the water was getting low. Gabriel used to say he never heard a frog croak afterwards without a sinking of the heart. It was the voice of misery. But Gabriel had strong partisans in this council. Le Maudit Pensonneau offered with his own hand to kill that interloping stranger whom he called the old devil, and argued the matter vehemently when his offer was declined. Le Maudit was a wild lad, so nervous that he stopped at nothing in his riding or his frolics; and so got the name of the Bewitched.[1]

But the third week, Gabriel said he had decided on a plan which might break off this detestable marriage if the others would help him. They all declared they would do anything for him, and he then told them he had privately sent word about it by Manette to Celeste; and Celeste was willing to have it or any plan attempted which would prevent the wedding.

"We will dress ourselves as Puants," said Gabriel, "and make a rush on the wedding party on the way to church, and carry off the bride."

Le Maudit Pensonneau sprung up and danced with joy when he heard that. Nothing would please him better than to dress as a Puant and carry off a bride. The Cahokians were so used to being raided by the Puants that they would readily believe such an attack had been made. That very week the Puants had galloped at midnight,

[1] Cahokian softening of cursed.

whooping through the town, and swept off from the common fields a flock of Le Page's goats and two of Larue's cattle. One might expect they would hear of such a wedding as Celeste Barbeau's. Indeed, the people were so tired of the Puants that they had sent urgently to St. Ange de Bellerive asking that soldiers be marched from Fort Chartres to give them military protection.

It would be easy enough for the young men to make themselves look like Indians. What one lacked another could supply.

"But two of us cannot take any part in the raid," said Gabriel. "Two must be ready at the river with a boat. And they must take Celeste as fast as they can row up the river to Pain Court to my aunt Choutou. My aunt Choutou will keep her safely until I can make some terms with Alexis Barbeau. Maybe he will give me his daughter, if I rescue her from the Puants. And if worst comes to worst, there is the missionary priest at Pain Court; he may be persuaded to marry us. But who is willing to be at the river?"

Paul and Jacques Le Page said they would undertake the boat. They were steady and trusty fellows and good river men; not so keen at riding and hunting as the others, but in better favor with the priest on account of their behavior.

So the scheme was very well laid out, and the wedding day came, clear and bright, as promising as any bride's day that ever was seen. Claudis Beauvois and a few of his friends galloped off to Prairie du Pont to bring the bride to church. The road from Caho' to Prairie du Pont was packed on both sides with dense thickets of black oak, honey locust, and red haws. Here and there a habitant had cut out a patch and built his cabin; or a path broken by hunters trailed towards the Mississippi. You ride the same track to-day, my child, only it is not as shaggy and savage as the course then lay.

And as soon as Claudis Beauvois was out of sight, Gabriel Chartrant followed with his dozen French Puants, in feathers and buckskin, all smeared with red and yellow ochre, well mounted and well armed. They rode along until they reached the last path which turns off to the river. At the end of that path, a mile away through the underbrush, Paul and Jacques Le Page were stationed with a boat. The young men with Gabriel dismounted and led their horses into the thicket to wait for his signal.

The birds had begun to sing just after three o'clock that clear morning, for Celeste lying awake heard them; and they were keeping it up in the bushes. Gabriel leaned his feathered head over the road, listening for hoof-falls and watching for the first puff of dust in the direction of Prairie du Pont. The road was not as well trodden as it is now, and a little ridge of weeds grew along the centre, high enough to rake the stirrup of a horseman.

But in the distance, instead of the pat-a-pat of iron hoofs began a sudden uproar of cries and wild whoops. Then a cloud of dust came in earnest. Claudis Beauvois alone, without any hat, wild with fright, was galloping towards Cahokia. Gabriel understood that something had happened which ruined his own plan. He and his men sprung on their horses and headed off the fugitive. The bridegroom who had passed that way so lately with smiles, yelled and tried to wheel his horse into the brush; but Gabriel caught his bridle and demanded to know what was the matter. As soon as he heard the French tongue spoken he begged for his life, and to know what more they required of him, since the rest of their band had already taken his bride. They made him tell them the facts. The real Puants had attacked the wedding procession before it was out of sight of Prairie du Pont, and had scattered it and carried off Celeste. He did not know what had become of anybody except himself, after she was taken.

Gabriel gave his horse a cut which was like a kick to its rider. He shot ahead, glad to pass what he had taken for a second body of Indians, and Le Maudit Pensonneau hooted after him.

"The miserable coward. I wish I had taken his scalp. He makes me feel a very good Puant indeed."

"Who cares what becomes of him?" said Gabriel. "It is Celeste that we want. The real Puants have got ahead of us and kidnaped the bride. Will any of you go with me?"

The poor fellow was white as ashes. Not a man needed to ask him where he was going, but they all answered in a breath and dashed after him. They broke directly through the thicket on the opposite side of the road, and came out into the tall prairie grass. They knew every path, marais, and rigolé for miles around, and took their course eastward, correctly judging that the Indians would follow the line of the bluffs and go north. Splash went their horses among the reeds of sloughs and across sluggish creeks, and by this short cut they soon came on the fresh trail.

At Falling Spring they made a halt to rest the horses a few minutes, and wash the red and yellow paint off their hands and faces; then galloped on along the rocky bluffs up the Bottom lands. But after a few miles they saw they had lost the trail. Closely scouting in every direction, they had to go back to Falling Spring, and there at last they found that the Indians had left the Bottom and by a winding path among rocks ascended to the uplands. Much time was lost. They had heard, while they galloped, the church bell tolling alarm in Cahokia, and they knew how the excitable inhabitants were running together at Beauvois' story, the women weeping and the men arming themselves, calling a council, and loading with contempt a runaway bridegroom.

Gabriel and his men, with their faces set north, hardly glanced aside to see the river shining along its distant bed. But one of them thought of saying, —

"Paul and Jacques will have a long wait with the boat."

The sun passed over their heads, and sunk hour by hour, and set. The western sky was red; and night began to close in, and still they urged their tired horses on. There would be a moon a little past its full, and they counted on its light when it should rise.

The trail of the Puants descended to the Bottom again at the head of the Grand Marais. There was heavy timber here. The night shadow of trees and rocks covered them, and they began to move more cautiously, for all signs pointed to a camp. And sure enough, when they had passed an abutment of the ridge, far off through the woods they saw a fire.

My son (mon Oncle Mathieu would say at this point of the story), will you do me the favor to bring me a coal for my pipe?

(The coal being brought in haste, he put it into the bowl with his finger and thumb, and seemed to doze while he drew at the stem. The smoke puffed deliberately from his lips, while all the time that mysterious fire was burning in the woods for my impatience to dance upon with hot feet, above the Grand Marais!)

Oh, yes, Gabriel and his men were getting very close to the Puants. They dismounted, and tied their horses in a crab-apple thicket and crept forward on foot. He halted them, and crawled alone toward the light to reconnoitre, careful not to crack a twig or make the least noise. The nearer he crawled the more his throat seemed to choke up and his ears to fill with buzzing sounds. The camp fire showed him Celeste tied to a tree. She looked pale and dejected, and her head rested against the tree stem, but her eyes kept roving the darkness in every direction as if she expected rescue. Her bridal finery had been torn by the bushes and her hair was loose, but Gabriel had never seen Celeste when she looked so beautiful.

Thirteen big Puants were sitting around the camp fire eating their supper of half-raw meat. Their horses were hobbled a little beyond, munching such picking as could be found among the fern. Gabriel went back as still as a snake and whispered his orders to his men.

Every Frenchman must pick the Puant directly in front of him, and be sure to hit that Puant. If the attack was half-hearted and the Indians gained time to rally, Celeste would suffer the consequences; they could kill her or escape with her. If you wish to gain an Indian's respect you must make a neat job of shooting him down. He never forgives a bungler.

"And then," said Gabriel, "we will rush in with our knives and hatchets. It must be all done in a moment."

The men reprimed their flintlocks, and crawled forward abreast. Gabriel was at the extreme right. When they were near enough he gave his signal, the nasal singing of the rattlesnake. The guns cracked all together, and every Cahokian sprung up to finish the work with knife and hatchet. Nine of the Puants fell dead, and the rest were gone before the smoke cleared. They left their meat, their horses, and arms. They were off like deer, straight through the woods to any place of safety. Every marksman had taken the Indian directly in front of him, but as they were abreast and the Puants in a circle, those four on the opposite side of the fire had been sheltered. Le Maudit Pensonneau scalped the red heads by the fire and hung the scalps in his belt. Our French people took up too easily, indeed, with savage ways; but Le Maudit Pensonneau was always full of his pranks.

Oh, yes, Gabriel himself untied Celeste. She was wild with joy, and cried on Gabriel's shoulder; and all the young men who had taken their first communion with Gabriel and had played with this dear girl when she was a child, felt the tears come into their own eyes. All but Le Maudit Pensonneau. He was busy rounding up the horses.

"Here's my uncle Larue's filly that was

taken two weeks ago," said Le Maudit, calling from the hobbling place. "And here are the blacks that Ferland lost, and Pierre's pony — half these horses are Caho' horses."

He tied them together so that they could be driven two or three abreast ahead of the party, and then he gathered up all the guns left by the Indians.

Gabriel now called a council, for it had to be decided directly what they should do next. Pain Court was seven miles in a straight line from the spot where they stood; while Cahokia was ten miles to the southwest.

"Would it not be best to go at once to Pain Court?" said Gabriel. "Celeste, after this frightful day, needs food and sleep as soon as she can get them, and my aunt Choutou is ready for her. And boats can always be found opposite Pain Court."

All the young men were ready to go to Pain Court. They really thought, even after all that had happened, that it would be wisest to deal with Alexis Barbeau at a distance. But Celeste herself decided the matter. Gabriel had not let go of her. He kept his hand on her as if afraid she might be kidnaped again.

"We will go home to my grandfather and grandmother au Caho'," said Celeste. "I will not go anywhere else."

"But you forget that Beauvois is au Caho'?" said one of the young men.

"Oh, I never can forget anything connected with this day," said Celeste, and the tears ran down her face. "I never can forget how willingly I let those Puants take me, and I laughed as one of them flung me on the horse behind him. We were nearly to the bluffs before I spoke. He did not say anything, and the others all had eyes which made me shudder. I pressed my hands on his buckskin sides and said to him, 'Gabriel.' And he turned and looked at me. I never had seen a feature of his frightful face before. And then I understood that the real Puants had me. Do you think I will ever marry anybody but the man who took me away from them? No. If worst comes to worst, I will go before the high altar and the image of the Holy Virgin, and make a public vow never to marry anybody else."

The young men flung up their arms in the air and raised a hurrah. Hats they had none to swing. Their cheeks were burnt by the afternoon sun. They were hungry and thirsty, and so tired that any one of them could have flung himself on the old leaves and slept as soon as he stretched himself. But it put new heart in them to see how determined she was.

So the horses were brought up, and the captured guns were packed upon some of the recovered ponies. There were some new blankets strapped on the backs of these Indian horses, and Gabriel took one of the blankets and secured it as a pillion behind his own saddle for Celeste to ride upon. As they rode out of the forest shadow they could see the moon just coming up over the hills beyond the great Cahokian mound.

It was midnight when the party trampled across the rigolé bridge into Cahokia streets. The people were sleeping with one eye open. All day, stragglers from the wedding procession had been coming in, and a company was organized for defense and pursuit. They had heard that the whole Pottawattamie nation had risen. And since Celeste Barbeau was kidnaped, anything might be expected. Gabriel and his men were missed early, but the excitement was so great that their unexplained absence was added without question to the general calamity. Candles showed at once, and men with gun barrels shining in the moonlight gathered quickly from all directions.

"Friends, friends!" Celeste called out; for the young men in buckskin, with their booty of driven horses, were enough like Puants to be in danger of a volley. "It is Celeste. Gabriel Chartrant and his men have killed the Indians and brought me back."

"It is Celeste Barbeau! Gabriel Chartrant and his men have killed the Indians and brought her back!" the word was passed on.

Her grandfather hung to her hand on one side of the horse, and her grandmother embraced her knees on the other. The old father was in his red nightcap and the old mother had pulled slippers on her bare feet. But without a thought of their appearance they wept aloud and fell on the neighbors' necks, and the neighbors fell upon each others' necks. Some kneeled down in the dust and returned thanks to the saints they had invoked. The auberge keeper and three old men who smoked their pipes steadily on his gallery every day took hold of hands and danced in a circle. Children who had waked to shriek with fear galloped the streets to proclaim at every window, "Celeste Barbeau is brought back!" The whole town was in a delirium of joy. Manette Le Compt, who had been brought home with the terrified bridesmaids and laughed in her sleeve all day because she thought Gabriel and his men were the Puants, leaned against a wall and turned sick. I have heard her say she never was so confused in her life as when she saw the driven horses, and the firearms, and those coarse-haired scalps hanging to Le Maudit Pensonneau's belt. The moon showed them all distinctly. Manette had thought it laughable when she heard that Alexis Barbeau was shut up in his brick house at Prairie du Pont, with all the men and guns he could muster to protect his property; but now she wept indignantly about it.

The priest had been the first man in the street, having lain down in all his clothes except his cassock, and he heartily gave Celeste and the young men his blessing, and counseled everybody to go to bed again. But Celeste reminded them that she was hungry, and as for the rescuers, they had ridden hard all day without a mouthful to eat. So the whole town made a feast, everybody bringing the best he had to Barbeau's house. They spread the table and crowded around, leaning over each other's shoulders to take up bits in their hands and eat with and talk to the young people. Gabriel's mother sat beside him with her arm around him, and opposite was Celeste with her grandfather and grandmother, and all the party were ranged around. The feathers had been blown out of their hair by that long chase, but their buckskins were soiled, and the hastily washed colors yet smeared their ears and necks. Yet this supper was quite like a bridal feast. Ah, my child, we never know it when we are standing in the end of the rainbow. Gabriel and Celeste might live a hundred years, but they could never be quite as happy again.

Paul and Jacques Le Page sat down with the other young men, and the noise of tongues in Barbeau's house could be heard out by the rigolé. It was like the swarming of wild bees. Paul and Jacques had waited with the boat until nightfall. They heard the firing when the Puants took Celeste, and watched hour after hour for some one to appear from the path; but at last concluding that Gabriel had been obliged to change his plan, they rowed back to Caho'.

Claudis Beauvois was the only person who did not sit up talking until dawn. And nobody thought about him until noon the next day, when Captain Jean Saucier with a company of fusileers rode into the village from Fort Chartres.

That was the first time my mother ever saw Captain Saucier. Your uncle François in Kaskaskia, he was also afterward Captain Saucier. I was not born until they had been married fifteen years. I was the last of their children. So Celeste Barbeau was kidnaped the day before my mother met my father.

Glad as the Cahokians were to see them, the troops were no longer needed, for the Puants had gone. They were frightened out of the country. Oh, yes, all those Indians wanted was a good whipping, and they got it. Alexis Barbeau had come along with the soldiers from Prairie du Pont, and he was not the only man who had made use of military escort. Basil Le Page had come up from New Orleans in the last fleet of pirogues to Kaskaskia. There he heard so much about the Puants that he bought a swift horse and armed himself for the ride northward, and was glad when he reached Fort Chartres to ride into Cahokia with Captain Saucier.

You might say Basil Le Page came in at one end of Cahokia and Claudis Beauvois went out at the other. For they knew one another directly, and it was noised in a minute that Basil said to his cousins Paul and Jacques : —

"What is that notorious swindler and gambler doing here? He left New Orleans suddenly, or he would be in prison now, and you will see if he stops here long after recognizing me."

Claudis Beauvois did not turn around in the street to look at any woman, rich or poor, when he left Cahokia, though how he left was not certainly known. Alexis Barbeau and his other associates knew better how their pockets were left.

Oh, yes, Alexis Barbeau was very willing for Celeste to marry Gabriel after that. He provided for them handsomely, and gave presents to each of the young men who had helped to take his daughter from the Puants; and he was so ashamed of the son-in-law he had wanted, that he never could endure to hear the man's name mentioned afterward. Alexis and the tavern-keeper used — when they were taking a social cup together — to hug each other without a word. The fine guest who had lived so long at the auberge and drank so much good wine, which was as fine as any in New Orleans, without expense, was as sore a memory to the poor landlord as to the rich landowner. But Celeste and Gabriel — my mother said when they were married the dancing and fiddling and feasting were kept up an entire week in Caho'.

PONTIAC'S LOOKOUT.

JENIEVE LALOTTE came out of the back door of her little house on Mackinac beach. The front door did not open upon either street of the village; and other domiciles were scattered with it along the strand, each little homestead having a front inclosure palisaded with oaken posts. Wooded heights sent a growth of bushes and young trees down to the pebble rim of the lake.

It had been raining, and the island was fresh as if new made. Boats and bateaux, drawn up in a great semicircle about the crescent bay, had also been washed; but they kept the marks of their long voyages to the Illinois Territory, or the Lake Superior region, or Canada. The very last of the winterers were in with their bales of furs, and some of these men were now roaring along the upper street in new clothes, exhilarated by spending on good cheer in one month the money it took them eleven months to earn. While in "hyvernements," or winter quarters, and on the long forest marches, the allowance of food per day, for a winterer, was one quart of corn and two ounces of tallow. On this fare the hardiest voyageurs ever known threaded a pathless continent and made a great traffic possible. But when they returned to the front of the world, — that distributing point in the straits, — they were fiercely importunate for what they considered the best the world afforded.

A segment of rainbow showed over one end of Round Island. The sky was dull rose, and a ship on the eastern horizon turned to a ship of fire, clean-cut and poised, a glistening object on a black bar of water. The lake was still, with blackness in its depths. The American flag on the fort rippled, a thing of living light, the stripes transparent. High pink clouds were riding down from the north, their flush dying as they piled aloft. There were shadings of peacock colors in the shoal water. Jenieve enjoyed this sunset beauty of the island, as she ran over the rolling pebbles, carrying some leather shoes by their leather strings. Her face was eager. She lifted the shoes to show them to three little boys playing on the edge of the lake.

"Come here. See what I have for you."

"What is it?" inquired the eldest, gazing betwixt the hairs scattered on his face; he stood with his back to the wind. His bare shins reddened in the wash of the lake, standing beyond its rim of shining gravel.

"Shoes," answered Jenieve, in a note triumphant over fate.

"What's shoes?" asked the smallest half-breed, tucking up his smock around his middle.

"They are things to wear on your feet," explained Jenieve; and her red-skinned half-brothers heard her with incredulity. She had told their mother, in their presence, that she intended to buy the children some shoes when she got pay for her spinning; and they thought it meant fashions from the Fur Company's store to wear to mass, but never suspected she had set her mind on dark-looking clamps for the feet.

"You must try them on," said Jenieve, and they all stepped experimentally from the water, reluctant to submit. But Jenieve was mistress in the house. There is no appeal from a sister who is a father to you, and even a substitute for your living mother.

"You sit down first, François, and wipe your feet with this cloth."

The absurdity of wiping his feet before he turned in for the night tickled François, though he was of a strongly aboriginal cast, and he let himself grin. Jenieve helped him struggle to encompass his lithe feet with the clumsy brogans.

"You boys are living like Indians."

"We are Indians," asserted François.

"But you are French, too. You are my brothers. I want you to go to mass looking as well as anybody."

Hitherto their object in life had been to escape mass. They objected to increasing their chances of church-going. Moccasins were the natural wear of human beings, and nobody but women needed even moccasins until cold weather. The proud look of an Iroquois taking spoils disappeared from the face of the youngest, giving way to uneasy anguish. The three boys sat down to tug, Jenieve going encouragingly from one to another. François lay on his back and pushed his heels skyward. Contempt and rebellion grew also in the faces of Gabriel and Toussaint. They were the true children of François Iroquois, her mother's second husband, who had been wont to lounge about Mackinac village in dirty buckskins and a calico shirt having one red and one blue sleeve. He had also bought a tall silk hat at the Fur Company's store, and he wore the hat under his blanket when it rained. If tobacco failed him, he scraped and dried willow peelings, and called them kinnickinnick. This worthy relation had worked no increase in Jenieve's home except an increase of children. He frequently yelled around the crescent bay, brandishing his silk hat in the exaltation of rum. And when he finally fell off the wharf into deep water, and was picked out to make another mound in the Indian burying-ground, Jenieve was so fiercely elated that she was afraid to confess it to the priest. Strange matches were made on the frontier, and Indian wives were commoner than any other kind; but through the whole mortifying existence of this Indian husband Jenieve avoided the sight of him, and called her mother steadily Mama Lalotte. The girl had remained with her grandmother, while François Iroquois carried off his wife to the Indian village on a western height of the island. Her grandmother had died, and Jenieve continued to keep house on the beach, having always with her one or more of the half-breed babies, until the plunge of François Iroquois allowed her to bring them all home with their mother. There was but one farm on the island, and Jenieve had all the spinning which the sheep afforded. She was the finest spinner in that region. Her grandmother had taught her to spin with a little wheel, as they still do about Quebec. Her pay was small. There was not much money then in the country, but bills of credit on the Fur Company's store were the same as cash, and she managed to feed her mother and the Indian's family. Fish were to be had for the catching, and she could get corn-meal and vegetables for her soup pot in partial exchange for her labor. The luxuries of life on the island were air and water, and the glories of evening and morning. People who could buy them got such gorgeous clothes as were brought by the Company. But usually Jenieve felt happy enough when she put on her best red homespun bodice and petticoat for mass or to go to dances. She did wish for shoes. The ladies at the fort had shoes, with heels which clicked when they danced. Jenieve could dance better, but she always felt their eyes on her moccasins, and came to regard shoes as the chief article of one's attire.

Though the joy of shoeing her brothers was not to be put off, she had not intended to let them keep on these precious brogans of civilization while they played beside the water. But she suddenly saw Mama Lalotte walking along the street near the lake with old Michel Pensonneau. Beyond these moving figures were many others, of engagés and Indians, swarming in front of the Fur Company's great warehouse. Some were talking and laughing; others were in a line, bearing bales of furs from bateaux just arrived at the log-and-stone wharf stretched from the centre of the bay. But all of them, and curious women peeping from their houses on the beach, particularly Jean Bati' McClure's wife, could see that Michel Pensonneau was walking with Mama Lalotte.

This sight struck cold down Jenieve's spine. Mama Lalotte was really the heaviest charge she had. Not twenty minutes before had that flighty creature been set to watch the supper pot, and here she was, mincing along, and fixing her pale blue laughing eyes on Michel Pensonneau, and bobbing her curly flaxen head at every word he spoke. A daughter who has a marrying mother on her hands may become morbidly anxious; Jenieve felt she should have no peace of mind during the month the coureurs-de-bois remained on the island. Whether they arrived early or late, they had soon to be off to the winter hunting-grounds; yet here was an emergency.

"Mama Lalotte!" called Jenieve. Her strong young fingers beckoned with authority. "Come here to me. I want you."

The giddy parent, startled and conscious, turned a conciliating smile that way. "Yes, Jenieve," she answered obediently, "I come." But she continued to pace by the side of Michel Pensonneau.

Jenieve desired to grasp her by the shoulder and walk her into the house; but when the world, especially Jean Bati' McClure's wife, is watching to see how you manage an unruly mother, it is necessary to use some adroitness.

"Will you please come here, dear Mama Lalotte? Toussaint wants you."

"No, I don't!" shouted Toussaint. "It is Michel Pensonneau I want, to make me some boats."

The girl did not hesitate. She intercepted the couple, and took her mother's arm in hers. The desperation of her act appeared to her while she was walking Mama Lalotte home; still, if nothing but force will restrain a parent, you must use force.

Michel Pensonneau stood squarely in his moccasins, turning redder and redder at the laugh of his cronies before the warehouse. He was dressed in new buckskins, and their tawny brightness made his florid cheeks more evident. Michel Pensonneau had been brought up by the Cadottes of Sault Ste. Marie, and he had rich relations at Cahokia, in the Illinois Territory. If he was not as good as the family of François Iroquois, he wanted to know the reason why. It is true, he was past forty and a bachelor. To be a bachelor, in that region, where Indian wives were so plenty and so easily got rid of, might bring some reproach on a man. Michel had begun to see that it did. He was an easy, gormandizing, good fellow, shapelessly fat, and he never had stirred himself during his month of freedom to do any courting. But Frenchmen of his class considered fifty the limit of an active life. It behooved him now to begin looking around; to prepare a fireside for himself. Michel was a good clerk to his employers. Cumbrous though his body might be, when he was in the woods he never shirked any hardship to secure a specially fine bale of furs.

Mama Lalotte, propelled against her will, sat down, trembling, in the house. Jenieve, trembling also, took the wooden bowls and spoons from a shelf and ladled out soup for the evening meal. Mama Lalotte was always willing to have the work done without trouble to herself, and she sat on a three-legged stool, like a guest. The supper pot boiled in the centre of the house, hanging on the crane which was fastened to a beam overhead. Smoke from the clear fire passed that richly darkened transverse of timber as it ascended, and escaped through a hole in the bark roof. The Fur Company had a great building with chimneys; but poor folks were glad to have a cedar hut of one room, covered with bark all around and on top. A fire-pit, or earthen hearth, was left in the centre, and the nearer the floor could be brought to this hole, without danger, the better the house was. On winter nights, fat French and half-breed children sat with heels to this sunken altar, and heard tales of massacre or privation which made the family bunks along the wall seem couches of luxury. It was the aboriginal hut patterned after his Indian brother's by the Frenchman; and the succession of British and American powers had not yet improved it. To Jenieve herself, the crisis before her, so insignificant against the background of that historic island, was more important than massacre or conquest.

"Mama,"— she spoke tremulously, — "I was obliged to bring you in. It is not proper to be seen on the street with an engagé. The town is now full of these bush-lopers."

"Bush-lopers, mademoiselle!" The little flaxen-haired woman had a shrill voice. "What was your own father?"

"He was a clerk, madame," maintained the girl's softer treble, "and always kept good credit for his family at the Company's store."

"I see no difference. They are all the same."

"François Iroquois was not the same." As the girl said this she felt a powder-like flash from her own eyes.

Mama Lalotte was herself a little ashamed of the François Iroquois alliance, but she answered, "He let me walk outside the house, at least. You allow me no amusement at all. I cannot even talk over the fence to Jean Bati' McClure's wife."

"Mama, you do not understand the danger of all these things, and I do. Jean Bati' McClure's wife will be certain to get you into trouble. She is not a proper woman for you to associate with. Her mind runs on nothing but match-making."

"Speak to her, then, for yourself. I wish you would get married."

"I never shall," declared Jenieve. "I have seen the folly of it."

"You never have been young," complained Mama Lalotte. "You don't know how a young person feels.

"I let you go to the dances," argued Jenieve. "You have as good a time as any woman on the island. But old Michel Pensonneau," she added sternly, "is not settling down to smoke his pipe for the remainder of his life on this doorstep."

"Monsieur Pensonneau is not old."

"Do you take up for him, Mama Lalotte, in spite of me?" In the girl's rich brunette face the scarlet of the cheeks deepened. "Am I not more to you than Michel Pensonneau or any other engagé? He is old; he is past forty. Would I call him old if he were no more than twenty?"

"Every one cannot be only twenty and a young agent," retorted her elder; and Jenieve's ears and throat reddened, also.

"Have I not done my best for you and the boys? Do you think it does not hurt me to be severe with you?"

Mama Lalotte flounced around on her stool, but made no reply. She saw peeping and smiling at the edge of the door a neighbor's face, that encouraged her insubordinations. Its broad, good-natured upper lip thinly veiled with hairs, its fleshy eyelids and thick brows, expressed a strength which she had not, yet would gladly imitate.

"Jenieve Lalotte," spoke the neighbor, "before you finish whipping your mother you had better run and whip the boys.

They are throwing their shoes in the lake."

"Their shoes!" Jenieve cried, and she scarcely looked at Jean Bati' McClure's wife, but darted outdoors along the beach.

"Oh, children, have you lost your shoes?"

"No," answered Toussaint, looking up with a countenance full of enjoyment.

"Where are they?"

"In the lake."

"You did n't throw your new shoes in the lake?"

"We took them for boats," said Gabriel freely. "But they are not even fit for boats."

"I threw mine as far as I could," observed François. "You can't make anything float in them."

She could see one of them stranded on the lake bottom, loaded with stones, its strings playing back and forth in the clear water. The others were gone out to the straits. Jenieve remembered all her toil for them, and her denial of her own wants that she might give to these half-savage boys, who considered nothing lost that they threw into the lake.

She turned around to run to the house. But there stood Jean Bati' McClure's wife, talking through the door, and encouraging her mother to walk with coureurs-de-bois. The girl's heart broke. She took to the bushes to hide her weeping, and ran through them towards the path she had followed so many times when her only living kindred were at the Indian village. The pine woods received her into their ascending heights, and she mounted towards sunset.

Panting from her long walk, Jenieve came out of the woods upon a grassy open cliff, called by the islanders Pontiac's Lookout, because the great war chief used to stand on that spot, forty years before, and gaze southward, as if he never could give up his hope of the union of his people. Jenieve knew the story. She had built playhouses here, when a child, without being afraid of the old chief's lingering influence; for she seemed to understand his trouble, and this night she was more in sympathy with Pontiac than ever before in her life. She sat down on the grass, wiping the tears from her hot cheeks, her dark eyes brooding on the lovely straits. There might be more beautiful sights in the world, but Jenieve doubted it; and a white gull drifted across her vision like a moving star.

Pontiac's Lookout had been the spot from which she watched her father's bateau disappear behind Round Island. He used to go by way of Detroit to the Canadian woods. Here she wept out her first grief for his death; and here she stopped, coming and going between her mother and grandmother. The cliff down to the beach was clothed with a thick growth which took away the terror of falling, and many a time Jenieve had thrust her bare legs over the edge to sit and enjoy the outlook.

There were old women on the island who could remember seeing Pontiac. Her grandmother had told her how he looked.

She had heard that, though his bones had been buried forty years beside the Mississippi, he yet came back to the Lookout every night during that summer month when all the tribes assembled at the island to receive money from a new government. He could not lie still while they took a little metal and ammunition in their hands in exchange for their country. As for the tribes, they enjoyed it. Jenieve could see their night fires begin to twinkle on Round Island and Bois Blanc, and the rising hubbub of their carnival came to her like echoes across the strait. There was one growing star on the long hooked reef which reached out from Round Island, and figures of Indians were silhouetted against the lake, running back and forth along that high stone ridge. Evening coolness stole up to Jenieve, for the whole water world was purpling; and sweet pine and cedar breaths, humid and invisible, were all around her. Her trouble grew small, laid against the granite breast of the island, and the woods darkened and sighed behind her. Jenieve could hear the shout of some Indian boy at the distant village. She was not afraid, but her shoulders contracted with a shiver. The place began to smell rankly of sweetbrier. There was no sweetbrier on the cliff or in the woods, though many bushes grew on alluvial slopes around the bay. Jenieve loved the plant, and often stuck a piece of it in her bosom. But this was a cold smell, striking chill to the bones. Her flesh and hair and clothes absorbed the scent, and it cooled her nostrils with its strange ether, the breath of sweetbrier, which always before seemed tinctured by the sun. She had a sensation of moving sidewise out of her own person; and then she saw the chief Pontiac standing on the edge of the cliff. Jenieve knew his back, and the feathers in his hair which the wind did not move. His head turned on a pivot, sweeping the horizon from St. Ignace, where the white man first set foot, to Round Island, where the shameful fires burned. His hard, set features were silver color rather than copper, as she saw his profile against the sky. His arms were folded in his blanket. Jenieve was as sure that she saw Pontiac as she was sure of the rock on which she sat. She poked one finger through the sward to the hardness underneath. The rock was below her, and Pontiac stood before her. He turned his head back from Round Island to St. Ignace. The wind blew against him, and the brier odor, sickening sweet, poured over Jenieve.

She heard the dogs bark in Mackinac village, and leaves moving behind her, and the wash of water at the base of the island which always sounded like a small rain. Instead of feeling afraid, she was in a nightmare of sorrow. Pontiac had loved the French almost as well as he loved his own people. She breathed the sweetbrier scent, her neck stretched forward and her dark eyes fixed on him; and as his head turned back from St. Ignace his whole body moved with it, and he looked at Jenieve.

His eyes were like a cat's in the purple

darkness, or like that heatless fire which shines on rotting bark. The hoar-frosted countenance was noble even in its most brutal lines. Jenieve, without knowing she was saying a word, spoke out: —

"Monsieur the chief Pontiac, what ails the French and Indians?"

"Malatat," answered Pontiac. The word came at her with force.

"Monsieur the chief Pontiac," repeated Jenieve, struggling to understand, "I say, what ails the French and Indians?"

"Malatat!" His guttural cry rang through the bushes. Jenieve was so startled that she sprung back, catching herself on her hands. But without the least motion of walking he was far westward, showing like a phosphorescent bar through the trees, and still moving on, until the pallor was lost from sight.

Jenieve at once began to cross herself. She had forgotten to do it before. The rankness of sweetbrier followed her some distance down the path, and she said prayers all the way home.

You cannot talk with great spirits and continue to chafe about little things. The boys' shoes and Mama Lalotte's lightness were the same as forgotten. Jenieve entered her house with dew in her hair, and an unterrified freshness of body for whatever might happen. She was certain she had seen Pontiac, but she would never tell anybody to have it laughed at. There was no candle burning, and the fire had almost died under the supper pot. She put a couple of sticks on the coals, more for their blaze than to heat her food. But the Mackinac night was chill, and it was pleasant to see the interior of her little home flickering to view. Candles were lighted in many houses along the beach, and amongst them Mama Lalotte was probably roaming, — for she had left the door open towards the lake, — and the boys' voices could be heard with others in the direction of the log wharf.

Jenieve took her supper bowl and sat down on the doorstep. The light cloud of smoke, drawn up to the roof-hole, ascended behind her, forming an azure gray curtain against which her figure showed, round-wristed and full-throated. The starlike camp fires on Round Island were before her, and the incessant wash of the water on its pebbles was company to her. Somebody knocked on the front door.

"It is that insolent Michel Pensonneau," thought Jenieve. "When he is tired he will go away." Yet she was not greatly surprised when the visitor ceased knocking and came around the palisades.

"Good-evening, Monsieur Crooks," said Jenieve.

"Good-evening, mademoiselle," responded Monsieur Crooks, and he leaned against the hut side, cap in hand, where he could look at her. He had never yet been asked to enter the house. Jenieve continued to eat her supper.

"I hope monsieur your uncle is well?"

"My uncle is well. It is n't necessary for me to inquire about madame your mother, for I have just seen her sitting on McClure's doorstep."

"Oh," said Jenieve.

The young man shook his cap in a restless hand. Though he spoke French easily, he was not dressed like an engagé, and he showed through the dark the white skin of the Saxon.

"Mademoiselle Jenieve,"—he spoke suddenly,—"you know my uncle is well established as agent of the Fur Company, and as his assistant I expect to stay here."

"Yes, monsieur. Did you take in some fine bales of furs to-day?"

"That is not what I was going to say."

"Monsieur Crooks, you speak all languages, don't you?"

"Not all. A few. I know a little of nearly every one of our Indian dialects."

"Monsieur, what does 'malatat' mean?"

"'Malatat'? That's a Chippewa word. You will often hear that. It means 'good for nothing.'"

"But I have heard that the chief Pontiac was an Ottawa."

The young man was not interested in Pontiac.

"A chief would know a great many dialects," he replied. "Chippewa was the tongue of this island. But what I wanted to say is that I have had a serious talk with the agent. He is entirely willing to have me settle down. And he says, what is the truth, that you are the best and prettiest girl at the straits. I have spoken my mind often enough. Why shouldn't we get married right away?"

Jenieve set her bowl and spoon inside the house, and folded her arms.

"Monsieur, have I not told you many times? I cannot marry. I have a family already."

The young agent struck his cap impatiently against the bark weather-boarding. "You are the most offish girl I ever saw. A man cannot get near enough to you to talk reason."

"It would be better if you did not come down here at all, Monsieur Crooks," said Jenieve. "The neighbors will be saying I am setting a bad example to my mother."

"Bring your mother up to the Fur Company's quarters with you, and the neighbors will no longer have a chance to put mischief into her head."

Jenieve took him seriously, though she had often suspected, from what she could see at the fort, that Americans had not the custom of marrying an entire family.

"It is really too fine a place for us."

Young Crooks laughed. Squaws had lived in the Fur Company's quarters, but he would not mention this fact to the girl.

His eyes dwelt fondly on her in the darkness, for though the fire behind her had again sunk to embers, it cast up a little glow; and he stood entirely in the star-embossed outside world. It is not safe to talk in the dark: you tell too much. The primitive instinct of truth-speaking revives in force, and the restraints of another's presence are gone. You speak from the unseen to the unseen over leveled barriers of reserve. Young Crooks had scarcely said that place was nothing, and he would rather live in that little house with Jenieve than in the Fur Company's quarters without her, when she exclaimed openly, "And have old Michel Pensonneau put over you!"

The idea of Michel Pensonneau taking precedence of him as master of the cedar hut was delicious to the American, as he recalled the engagé's respectful slouch while receiving the usual bill of credit.

"One may laugh, monsieur. I laugh myself; it is better than crying. But it is the truth that Mama Lalotte is more care to me than all the boys. I have no peace except when she is asleep in bed."

"There is no harm in Madame Lalotte."

"You are right, monsieur. Jean Bati' McClure's wife puts all the mischief in her head. She would even learn to spin, if that woman would let her alone."

"And I never heard any harm of Michel Pensonneau. He is a good enough fellow, and he has more to his credit on the Company's books than any other engagé now on the island."

"I suppose you would like to have him sit and smoke his pipe the rest of his days on your doorstep?"

"No, I wouldn't," confessed the young agent. "Michel is a saving man, and he uses very mean tobacco, the cheapest in the house."

"You see how I am situated, monsieur. It is no use to talk to me."

"But Michel Pensonneau is not going to trouble you long. He has relations at Cahokia, in the Illinois Territory, and he is fitting himself out to go there to settle."

"Are you sure of this, monsieur?"

"Certainly I am, for we have already made him a bill of credit to our correspondent at Cahokia. He wants very few goods to carry across the Chicago portage."

"Monsieur, how soon does he intend to go?"

"On the first schooner that sails to the head of the lake; so he may set out any day. Michel is anxious to try life on the Mississippi, and his three years' engagement with the Company is just ended."

"I also am anxious to have him try life on the Mississippi," said Jenieve, and she drew a deep breath of relief. "Why did you not tell me this before?"

"How could I know you were interested in him?"

"He is not a bad man," she admitted kindly. "I can see that he means very well. If the McClures would go to the Illinois Territory with him — But, Monsieur Crooks," Jenieve asked sharply, "do people sometimes make sudden marriages?"

"In my case they have not," sighed the young man. "But I think well of sudden marriages myself. The priest comes to the island this week."

"Yes, and I must take the children to confession."

"What are you going to do with me, Jenieve?"

"I am going to say good-night to you, and shut my door." She stepped into the house.

"Not yet. It is only a little while since

they fired the sunset gun at the fort. You are not kind to shut me out the moment I come."

She gave him her hand, as she always did when she said good-night, and he prolonged his hold of it.

"You are full of sweetbrier. I didn't know it grew down here on the beach."

"It never did grow here, Monsieur Crooks."

"You shall have plenty of it in your garden, when you come home with me."

"Oh, go away, and let me shut my door, monsieur. It seems no use to tell you I cannot come."

"No use at all. Until you come, then, good-night."

Seldom are two days alike on the island. Before sunrise the lost dews of paradise always sweeten those scented woods, and the birds begin to remind you of something you heard in another life, but have forgotten. Jenieve loved to open her door and surprise the east. She stepped out the next morning to fill her pail. There was a lake of translucent cloud beyond the water lake: the first unruffled, and the second wind-stirred. The sun pushed up, a flattened red ball, from the lake of steel ripples to the lake of calm clouds. Nearer, a schooner with its sails down stood black as ebony between two bars of light drawn across the water, which lay dull and bleak towards the shore. The addition of a schooner to the scattered fleet of sailboats, bateaux, and birch canoes made Jenieve laugh. It must have arrived from Sault Ste. Marie in the night. She had hopes of getting rid of Michel Pensonneau that very day. Since he was going to Cahokia, she felt stinging regret for the way she had treated him before the whole village; yet her mother could not be sacrificed to politeness. Except his capacity for marrying, there was really no harm in the old fellow, as Monsieur Crooks had said.

The humid blockhouse and walls of the fort high above the bay began to glisten in emerging sunlight, and Jenieve determined not to be hard on Mama Lalotte that day. If Michel came to say good-by, she would shake his hand herself. It was not agreeable for a woman so fond of company to sit in the house with noboby but her daughter. Mama Lalotte did not love the pine woods, or any place where she would be alone. But Jenieve could sit and spin in solitude all day, and think of that chill silver face she had seen at Pontiac's Lookout, and the floating away of the figure, a phosphorescent bar through the trees, and of that spoken word which had denounced the French and Indians as good for nothing. She decided to tell the priest, even if he rebuked her. It did not seem any stranger to Jenieve than many things which were called natural, such as the morning miracles in the eastern sky, and the growth of the boys, her dear torments. To Jenieve's serious eyes, trained by her grandmother, it was not as strange as the sight of Mama Lalotte, a child in maturity, always craving amusement, and easily led by any chance hand.

The priest had come to Mackinac in the schooner during the night. He combined this parish with others more or less distant, and he opened the chapel and began his duties as soon as he arrived. Mama Lalotte herself offered to dress the boys for confession. She put their best clothes on them, and then she took out all her own finery. Jenieve had no suspicion while the little figure preened and burnished itself, making up for the lack of a mirror by curves of the neck to look itself well over. Mama Lalotte thought a great deal about what she wore. She was pleased, and her flaxen curls danced. She kissed Jenieve on both cheeks, as if there had been no quarrel, though unpleasant things never lingered in her memory. And she made the boys kiss Jenieve; and while they were saddened by clothes, she also made them say they were sorry about the shoes.

By sunset, the schooner, which had sat

in the straits all day, hoisted its sails and rounded the hooked point of the opposite island. The gun at the fort was like a parting salute, and a shout was raised by coureurs-de-bois thronging the log wharf. They trooped up to the fur warehouse, and the sound of a fiddle and the thump of soft-shod feet were soon heard; for the French were ready to celebrate any occasion with dancing. Laughter and the high excited voices of women also came from the little ball-room, which was only the office of the Fur Company.

Here the engagés felt at home. The fiddler sat on the top of the desk, and men lounging on a row of benches around the walls sprang to their feet and began to caper at the violin's first invitation. Such maids and wives as were nearest the building were haled in, laughing, by their relations; and in the absence of the agents, and of that awe which goes with making your crossmark on a paper, a quick carnival was held on the spot where so many solemn contracts had been signed. An odor of furs came from the packing-rooms around, mixed with gums and incense-like whiffs. Added to this was the breath of the general store kept by the agency. Tobacco and snuff, rum, chocolate, calico, blankets, wood and iron utensils, fire-arms, West India sugar and rice, — all sifted their invisible essences on the air. Unceiled joists showed heavy and brown overhead. But there was no fireplace, for when the straits stood locked in ice and the island was deep in snow, no engagé claimed admission here. He would be a thousand miles away, toiling on snow-shoes with his pack of furs through the trees, or bargaining with trappers for his contribution to this month of enormous traffic.

Clean buckskin legs and brand-new belted hunting-shirts whirled on the floor, brightened by sashes of crimson or kerchiefs of orange. Indians from the reservation on Round Island, who happened to be standing, like statues, in front of the building, turned and looked with lenient eye on the performance of their French brothers. The fiddler was a nervous little Frenchman with eyes like a weasel, and he detected Jenieve Lalotte putting her head into the room. She glanced from figure to figure of the dancers, searching through the twilight for what she could not find; but before he could call her she was off. None of the men, except a few Scotch-French, were very tall, but they were a handsome, muscular race, fierce in enjoyment, yet with a languor which prolonged it, and gave grace to every picturesque pose. Not one of them wanted to pain Lalotte's girl, but, as they danced, a joyful fellow would here and there spring high above the floor and shout, "Good voyage to Michel Pensonneau and his new family!" They had forgotten the one who amused them yesterday, and remembered only the one who amused them to-day.

Jenieve struck on Jean Bati' McClure's door, and faced his wife, speechless, pointing to the schooner ploughing southward.

"Yes, she's gone," said Jean Bati' McClure's wife, "and the boys with her."

The confidante came out on the step, and tried to lay her hand on Jenieve's shoulder, but the girl moved backward from her.

"Now let me tell you, it is a good thing for you, Jenieve Lalotte. You can make a fine match of your own to-morrow. It is not natural for a girl to live as you have lived. You are better off without them."

"But my mother has left me!"

"Well, I am sorry for you; but you were hard on her."

"I blame you, madame!"

"You might as well blame the priest, who thought it best not to let them go unmarried. And she has taken a much worse man than Michel Pensonneau in her time."

"My mother and my brothers have left me here alone," repeated Jenieve; and she wrung her hands and put them over her face. The trouble was so overwhelming that it broke her down before her enemy.

"Oh, don't take it to heart," said Jean Bati' McClure's wife, with ready interest in the person nearest at hand. "Come and eat supper with my man and me to-night, and sleep in our house if you are afraid."

Jenieve leaned her forehead against the hut, and made no reply to these neighborly overtures.

"Did she say nothing at all about me, madame?"

"Yes; she was afraid you would come at the last minute and take her by the arm and walk her home. You were too strict with her, and that is the truth. She was glad to get away to Cahokia. They say it is fine in the Illinois Territory. You know she is fond of seeing the world."

The young supple creature trying to restrain her shivers and sobs of anguish against the bark house side was really a moving sight; and Jean Bati' McClure's wife, flattening a masculine upper lip with resolution, said promptly, —

"I am going this moment to the Fur Company's quarters to send young Monsieur Crooks after you."

At that Jenieve fled along the beach and

took to the bushes. As she ran, weeping aloud like a child, she watched the lessening schooner; and it seemed a monstrous thing, out of nature, that her mother was on that little ship, fleeing from her, with a thoughtless face set smiling towards a new world. She climbed on, to keep the schooner in sight, and made for Pontiac's Lookout, reckless of what she had seen there.

The distant canvas became one leaning sail, and then a speck, and then nothing. There was an afterglow on the water which turned it to a wavering pavement of yellow-pink sheen. In that clear, high atmosphere, mainland shores and islands seemed to throw out the evening purples from themselves, and thus to slowly reach for one another and form darkness. Jenieve had lain on the grass, crying, "O Mama — François — Toussaint — Gabriel!" But she sat up at last, with her dejected head on her breast, submitting to the pettiness and treachery of what she loved. Bats flew across the open place. A sudden rankness of sweetbrier, taking her breath away by its icy puff, reminded her of other things, and she tried to get up and run. Instead of running she seemed to move sidewise out of herself, and saw Pontiac standing on the edge of the cliff. His head turned from St. Ignace to the reviving fires on Round Island, and slowly back again from Round Island to St. Ignace. Jenieve felt as if she were choking, but again she asked out of her heart to his, —

"Monsieur the chief Pontiac, what ails the French and Indians?"

He floated around to face her, the high ridges of his bleached features catching light; but this time he showed only dim dead eyes. His head sunk on his breast, and Jenieve could see the fronds of the feathers he wore traced indistinctly against the sky. The dead eyes searched for her and could not see her; he whispered hoarsely to himself, "Malatat!"

The voice of the living world calling her name sounded directly afterwards in the woods, and Jenieve leaped as if she were shot. She had the instinct that her lover must not see this thing, for there were reasons of race and religion against it. But she need not have feared that Pontiac would show himself, or his long and savage mourning for the destruction of the red man, to any descendant of the English. As the bushes closed behind her she looked back: the phosphoric blur was already so far in the west that she could hardly be sure she saw it again. And the young agent of the Fur Company, breaking his way among leaves, met her with both hands; saying gayly, to save her the shock of talking about her mother: —

"Come home, come home, my sweetbrier maid. No wonder you smell of sweetbrier. I am rank with it myself, rubbing against the dewy bushes."

www.ingramcontent.com/pod-product-compliance
Lightning Source LLC
Chambersburg PA
CBHW032141230426
43672CB00011B/2408